I'm Lonely, LORD— How Long?

THE PSALMS FOR TODAY

Marva J. Dawn

1817

Harper & Row, Publishers, San Francisco

Cambridge, Hagerstown, New York, Philadelphia
London, Mexico City, São Paulo, Sydney

FIRST EDITION

Designer: Jim Mennick

Library of Congress Cataloging in Publication Data

Dawn, Marva J.
    I'M LONELY, LORD—HOW LONG?

    Bibliography: p.
    1. Bible. O.T. Psalms—Meditations. 2. Loneliness—Religious aspects—Christianity—Meditations.
I. Title.
BS1430.4.S42   242'.5   83–47721
ISBN 0–06–067201–3

---

84 85 86 87 10 9 8 7 6 5 4 3 2 1

To Nancy,

whose prayers helped this book to come into existence,
whose life enfolds everyone around her in the love of God,
whose battle against leukemia has also been a means for glorifying God.

Contents

Preface   *ix*

1. I'm Lonely, LORD—How Long?   *1*

2. The LORD Is in Control of Time   *7*

3. God Hears My Cries of Panic   *13*

4. My Trust Won't Put Me to Shame   *19*

5. God's Mother-Love   *25*

6. Lonely and Afflicted—But Yahweh Releases Me from the Snare   *31*

7. Yahweh Understands Even Betrayal   *36*

8. Evening, Morning, and Noon, He Hears My Voice   *42*

9. It's All Right to Be Afraid   *48*

10. Our God Records Our Tears   *54*

11. The Right Kind of Fear   *59*

12. Joy When Nothing Seems to Be Good   *66*

13. The Right Kind of Boasting   *72*

14. Radiance and Angels   *77*

15. Tasting the LORD's Goodness   *82*

16. The LORD Is Near When We've Lost All Hope   *89*

17. I Thought I Would Die, But the LORD Helped   *95*

18. The Wicked Aren't So Fat and Sleek   *101*

19. In Our Brutishness, God Holds Our Hand   *107*

20. To Desire Nothing On Earth   *113*

21. Even in Death the LORD Protects Us   *118*

22. Lest We Forget That We Are Special   *125*

23. Help to Resist Temptation   *131*

24. God Sets the Lonely in Families   *137*

25. Worship Really Matters   *143*

26. Finding the Strength to Go On   *149*

27. Comfort Even When There Is No Assurance   *156*

28. Putting Our Grief into Historical Perspective   *163*

29. The LORD Will Give Us the Desires of Our Hearts   *170*

30. When I Fret and Fall, There Is *Shalom*   *176*

31. So Now I Can't Keep It to Myself   *182*

Appendix A. Swimming the Psalms   *191*

Appendix B. When Is a Rut Not a Rut?
           Hidden Promise in Psalm 23   *197*

List of Resources   *201*

Subject Index   *203*

Scripture Index   *207*

Preface

I was born a fighter. I grew up in a family that reacted to financial struggles, to the pressures of teaching, and to the rigors of administering a large parochial school with hard work. They modeled the good fight of faith. My learning to fight in faith was positive; my difficulties have arisen when I've thought I could, by virtue of my own power and intellect, control the circumstances of life.

That faith which had developed throughout my childhood sustained me when, at the age of sixteen, I watched my whole world crash. I couldn't recover from a seemingly mild case of measles at the end of my sophomore year of high school. Once a rowdy child and then an eager athlete, I began to lose weight and strength and, by Christmas of my junior year, was reduced to a mere skeleton of my former self. But the measles virus that had evidently destroyed my pancreas, necessitating a lifelong battle against the escalating effects of diabetes, also brought me closer to the Lord; and succeeding crashes related to my health have repeatedly tested and strengthened my fight of faith.

Following my graduation from high school, I went first to a Lutheran teachers college, where I majored in English and theology and minored in music and secondary education, and then to the University of Idaho in Moscow to do an M.A. in English—fully intending to go on to England to get a Ph.D. and return to teach in a Lutheran college somewhere. But two major events interrupted those plans.

Because of my double major in college, I was able to create and teach a course in Literature of the Bible at Idaho and thereby discover that my real love in life is teaching the Scriptures. Also, I met a man there who became my husband. Remaining in Moscow after marriage, I enjoyed immensely my work in a church's educational and music programs and my responsibility for that church's campus ministry at the University of Idaho and Washington State University.

When my husband's new job took us to Olympia, I found it terribly difficult to leave the work in which I was so happy. Although I had a hard time finding myself after the move, once again the old fighting instinct took over. I went back to school in theology, and eventually I began to work on the pastoral staff of a Lutheran church while finishing my M.Div. degree. Once again I found great joy in my work; once again my life was ripped apart—this time by a crash more severe than any health problem: my husband left me and married one of the members of the church youth group. This time there was no power, no intellectual answers, to cope with the devastation. I fought the pain and despair by pouring myself into my work.

The grace of God rescued me at that time through the founding of "C.E.M.: Christians Equipped for Ministry." Under the care of seven families on the board of directors, this corporation has enabled me to work for the last four years as a free-lance Bible teacher—speaking for conventions, leading retreats and Bible conferences, writing books.

Almost a year after my husband left me, God provided the finances for an old three-story house, with room for my housemate Julie's art studio on the top floor and my office in the basement, and with five bedrooms to give us space for ministering to women in crisis. C.E.M. hired a director for that EPHESUS House ministry, and we learned many valuable lessons during the months that we had guests in our home. When the director went back to school, I tried unsuccessfully to carry on that ministry, along with my teaching and writing. I soon learned the limitations of my gifts.

Julie and I searched for other ways to use our big house, and finally the Carson family of four joined us to create a Christian community. After several months together, our household is splitting up now, as I prepare to leave for the University of Notre Dame to finish my Ph.D., and Julie prepares for her marriage.

To keep my diabetes under control the past few years, I've been swimming at least a mile three or four times a week. This has built up my strength and endurance and provided precious time for prayer and meditation. The discipline has thus brought great physical, emotional, and spiritual healing.

At times, however, I get very discouraged by my constant

struggle for health. In the last nine months, I've had two major surgeries (a hysterectomy and emergency surgery to remove fifteen inches of intestine that had intussuscepted and strangled itself) and two minor surgeries (to remove a cherry angiometa on my arm and to release a trigger finger); I've spent three weeks and then six weeks on crutches because I'm so susceptible to gangrene when I injure or burn my feet; I constantly battle glare problems and limited vision due to advancing cataracts; hills—even stairs—are hard to climb because my blood vessels can't carry energy and oxygen well enough; exercising causes much pain because those same blood vessels can't carry away the carbon dioxide effectively; periodontal problems require painful gum massage and scraping every night; and every day is a struggle to balance the amount of insulin I inject with diet and exercise. Some days I'm really tired of all the strain.

Most days my reaction to pain is to fight. I read, work on my writing, get ready for the next speaking engagement, swim harder and longer.

I'm not claiming that my method of coping with problems has any great merit. In fact, it has serious flaws. But it explains some of the stories in the pages that follow. And as I learn to believe more deeply in the God of the Scriptures that are expounded on these pages, I will learn better methods for dealing with life's problems—methods of trust and rest.

Since I've been alone, I've resorted to familiar coping patterns—fighting physical limitations with a rigorous discipline of body, pushing myself to be as capable as possible, fighting the ravages of divorce with a rigorous discipline of work, seeking wholeness in serving others. But how does one fight the attacks of loneliness that work on us doubly because all the other battles have to be fought alone? I struggle with my desire to be loved and dread the loneliness of bus stations and long hours of solitary work.

My major equipment for that fight is the Scriptures. In the Psalms, especially, God reveals himself to us as one who cares about our pain and sustains us in it. I want to learn better to trust him so that, instead of trying to fight my battle alone, I can rest in his fight for me and appreciate the gifts he gives to free me from my loneliness.

I'm grateful to the friends who have helped to bring healing to my life—particularly those who have allowed me to include them in the stories of this book.

Also, I thank especially my editor, Roy M. Carlisle of Harper & Row San Francisco, who cared enough about the subject matter of this book to be patient with me in working on it, and the members of the C.E.M. Board, who believed in me when I couldn't.

1. I'm Lonely, LORD— How Long?

How long, O LORD? Will you forget me forever?
　How long will you hide your face from me?
How long must I wrestle with my thoughts
　and every day have sorrow in my heart?
　How long will my enemy triumph over me?
Look on me and answer, O LORD my God.
　Give light to my eyes, or I will sleep in death,
my enemy will say, "I have overcome him,"
　and my foes will rejoice when I fall.
But I trust in your unfailing love;
　my heart rejoices in your salvation.
I will sing to the LORD,
　for he has been good to me.

Psalm 13*

How long, O LORD? How long must I stare at this typewriter and remain blocked in my efforts to get past the failures of my own life?

An overwhelming number of us are lonely—coming out of (or maybe just beginning to go into) terrible times of rejection or crisis or fear. Sometimes we are lonely for a specific reason: our spouse has recently died or left us; our children have just gone from home; we are fighting a particular battle against illness; we are new in the neighborhood; our values are different from those of our work colleagues; it is a Friday night and all our other single friends have dates. Sometimes our loneliness is a general, pervasive alienation: we just don't feel as if we belong in our place of work, in our neighborhood, in our family, even in our church. Maybe we don't have anyone with whom we can share all the dimensions of our lives.

We need good news that isn't just trite folk wisdom slapped

---

* All Biblical passages used are taken from the New International Version unless otherwise indicated.

on superficially in a meaningless attempt to help us feel better. Yet, after all my preparations, translating Hebrew passages and meditating on the Psalms and gathering their words of comfort, my writing has been blocked by the very "how long?" syndrome that the Scriptures intend to counteract.

In that syndrome we think that as soon as circumstances in our lives get right, we can proceed. When they don't, we remain incapacitated and ask, "How long, LORD?"

In our loneliness, especially, we join the psalmist to ask God if he is going to forget us forever. The Hebrew text literally says, "an everlastingness." God seems to have dropped us out of his plans. Nothing is changing. We have been abandoned.

David, the writer of Psalm 13, is gutsy and honest. We are comforted to know that he struggled with the "how long?" syndrome as we do. His honesty, further, invites us to be real about our emotions as he is. When we feel that God has abandoned us, sometimes we act as though we would sin even more by being real with God about the vacuum we are feeling. He already knows how we feel, so we might as well not compound our problems by being dishonest about them.

The second "how long?" question elaborates on the reason that we feel abandoned by God. The poet asks how long the LORD will hide from him his face. That Old Testament idiom means to withhold one's kindness or, even more painful, to withdraw it.

When we are suffering from acute loneliness, it seems that God has pulled back his love. He doesn't seem to want us to recover. If he did, we think, he would send whatever is necessary to ease our pain and fix things up.

In the heartbreak of divorce I kept wishing that perhaps someday somebody would love me so much that he would ease my loneliness forever. If God really loved me, it seemed he would send such a person.

Whatever the reason, we've all probably felt this way at times: Why does the LORD hold back his love? Must he punish us for some reason? How long must this punishment, this denial of our "needs," go on?

The psalmist continues by asking how long he must continue to wrestle with his thoughts. The phrase "every day" in the next line occurs at the end of the sentence in the Hebrew text and might better be rendered "all the day." One commentator suggests, then, that the expression, "all the night," might be presupposed for the line about thought-wrestling, to complete the pattern.* Our own experience confirms such a possibility for the text. I'm sure you have stayed awake all night trying to plan ways to end your pain. When I am excruciatingly lonely, I can usually hide it from myself during the day by being busy at work, and I can find comfort by crying with friends who care. But after I get into bed, I ache with the emptiness. Too many nights I have turned increasingly inward to hide from the loneliness that engulfs me. I have tried to manipulate life so that I can either eliminate the pain or become numb to it.

However, as the poet continues, we realize that those plans of the night don't usually work out. Though he gives no specifics, David's enemies were the ones to frustrate his plans. In fact, such anguish is caused by his enemies that David fears for his life (vv. 3–4).

In the twentieth century, our enemies are not usually people trying to harm us physically. We must put the meaning of this psalm into our modern experience and apply it to the enemies that seem to triumph over us today. Who or what are they for you?

Your enemies might be individual people: malicious gossips or faultfinders criticizing your work or blaming you for a divorce. Perhaps your adversaries are financial problems or the lack of a home in which to find some sense of belonging and security. Maybe your foes are various fears for the future or pains from the rejections of the past.

Whether persons, things, or attitudes, our enemies immobilize us. We get too nervous meeting new people because we fear their rejection. We assume we're ugly when no one asks us for a date. Sometimes we worry so much about how to find enough to do to fill up all our time alone that we are unable to do anything. Or we do not know how to reach out to new workers in our office because we feel so fragmented from our divorce. We are unable to be open to feelings because previous

---

* H. C. Leupold, *Exposition of Psalms* (reprint, Grand Rapids, Mich.: Baker Book House, 1969), p. 135.

risks have brought too much pain. How long, LORD, must we be helpless in the face of these enemies?

"But I trust in your unfailing love." After all the discouraged "how long?" questions, suddenly the psalmist is writing words of hope and victory. The key lies in one of my favorite Hebrew words, the noun *chesedh,* which is translated "unfailing love" in the New International Version of Psalm 13. The term describes the steadfast, covenant love of Yahweh, the amazing grace of his infinite kindness and compassion toward us, his people.

This word answers the first and second questions of the psalm. The unfailing steadfastness of *chesedh* tells us for sure that God has not forgotten us, not for a moment; nor will he ever.

Chesedh also answers the third "how long?" The nature of *chesedh* is that God will never withdraw his support from us. It may seem so when he does not grant us what we ask, but in his infinite wisdom and love he is always answering according to what really is best for us.

Of course, it will seem that we wrestle with our thoughts for too long. As long as we are depending upon our own thoughts, the anguish will continue. Only when we are finally reduced to the point of helplessness, the realization that we will never be able to deal with our loneliness by ourselves, will we give in to *chesedh* and let God bring to us the gifts of his love. When we participate in his plans willingly, we can discover the Joy of them.

I have been capitalizing the word *Joy* for years to distinguish it from merely human happinesses. There are times when our circumstances make happiness impossible, but we can always experience profound Joy when we are aware that in his *chesedh* God is able to transform even the direst of circumstances. (This will be explained more thoroughly on page 68.)

We dare not be superficial about this and say, "Oh, yes, God loves you; therefore, you *ought* to be happy." When others dump the gospel on us like that, not only are we not comforted, but our guilt is compounded because we believe (falsely) that Christians should be able to answer that *ought* by cranking up the better feelings.

The essence of the matter is that we can't experience the truth of *chesedh* in the reality of our feelings until we know it first as a fact of faith. We still wonder how long, yet deep underneath we are convinced that ultimately *chesedh* reigns because that is the way God has always dealt with his people. Surely, he will not single us out as individuals to withhold from us his *chesedh*. In that fact we can trust, even before it has sunk into our feelings.

Sometimes it helps, the psalmist points out, to look back to the past. The final verse says, "I will sing because the LORD has been good to me." Not only will we be able someday to sing because we will have learned how he has been good to us in this situation, but also right now we can sing because he has been good to us in the past.

Do you remember times when you felt you couldn't go on because the loneliness was so devastating? Then, at just the right time, God sent his love in some special way—a phone call or a hug from someone special, a good book that brought his *chesedh* into your conscious thought. We can train our minds to turn to memories of those times in the moments when we are tempted to ask, "How long?" and, thus, be strengthened by the precious instances when the "how long?" came crashing to a halt in the wonder of God's *chesedh*.

That is why the psalmist can say, "My heart rejoices in your salvation." The Hebrew language doesn't have past, present, or future tense verbs as our English does. Its verbs indicate simply completed or incompleted action. The verb here about rejoicing is in the imperfect, or incomplete, form. We could translate it, "My heart will rejoice in your salvation," or, as in the NIV above, "My heart rejoices" (the action is still going on). If we are not experiencing Joy in God's deliverance yet, we can confidently look forward to the time when we will. Furthermore, that very assurance that his *chesedh* will not fail us, that some day he will come through with deliverance, enables us to rejoice now in the meantime.

The delightful irony is that usually the change of attitude is the deliverance. As soon as we stop asking, "How long?" we are liberated from that question's bondage. Then we can rejoice instead in the memories of how God has been good to us or

"how bountifully He has dealt" with us (the New American
Standard Version).

That is how it is here at my desk. I don't have to stare at the
typewriter until my loneliness problems are solved. Psalm 13
frees my fingers and heart from the immobility and anguish of
"how long?" I don't feel alone right now. I feel Joy in your
company as we share the deep awareness that the *chesedh* of the
LORD our God is great enough to warrant our trust.

FOR FURTHER MEDITATION

The following suggestions for reflection can provide connec-
tions between the principles discovered in our intensive Bible
study and the daily particulars of your own discipleship. These
might help you to apply the ideas of each chapter to the work
of your day, to prepare for future discussion if you are using
this book for study in a group, and to link what God is teaching
you through the Psalms with how you respond to him and
reach out to others around you.

1. What kinds of experiences cause me to think that God has
   forgotten me?
2. What gifts do I think he should have given me, but he
   hasn't?
3. When do I get caught in wrestling with my own thoughts
   and plans?
4. Who or what are the enemies that frustrate my plans?
5. How can I see that God enables me to triumph over those
   enemies?
6. What are some examples of his *chesedh* in action in my life?
7. Am I able to rejoice in his deliverance yet? Why, or why not?

2. The LORD Is in Control of Time

But I trust in you, O LORD;
I say, "You are my God."
My times are in your hands.
Psalm 31:14–15a

Suppose you have two kinds of friends. One kind is not very reliable. Just when you count on them, they let you down. If you reveal to them your deepest inmost secrets, they either laugh at you or tell everybody else.

Your other friends are made of solid rock. You know that you can confide in them and they will be true to you, no matter what. You can count on them in any circumstance; they will stand by you or else be honest about why they can't.

To which kind of friend will you turn in a crisis? Which one will you trust?

Exactly. You will turn to the one who is trustable, the one who is worthy of your confidence. Your trusting will not depend upon how good you are at trusting, but upon your knowledge that the one on whom you lean is stable and will assuredly support you.

That is the necessary basis for this chapter's discussion of our "times." In fact, it is the basis for all of this book. The psalmist David declares that it is the LORD, Yahweh, in whom he trusts. We must therefore, first of all, consider who Yahweh is.

The difference between LORD, Lord, and lord in most translations of the Old Testament tells us which Hebrew word underlies the English rendering. If the Hebrew word is *Yahweh,* then all the letters are capitalized. If it is *adonai,* a word that means "master" or "ruler," then only its first letter is capitalized when it refers to God, and it is left lowercase when it refers to human masters.

Throughout the Old Testament, God continually reveals to

the Children of Israel new dimensions of the meaning of his name. Then, when Jesus comes in the New Testament, he claims that "I AM"-ness for himself and demonstrates in human form for all to see what the character of God is like. He shows us his tender love, his infinite care, his overwhelming patience.

On the basis of God's thorough revelation, we can, throughout this study of God's comfort for our loneliness, come back again and again to the fact that God is called by the name, *Yahweh.* He is the Covenant God, the one who has never broken any of his promises. He is the faithful, loving, holy, just, steadfast, compassionate, creative One whose infinite majesty and sovereignty we can never comprehend. Yet the more we search to know who he is, the more we will be able to trust him.

If we have learned that he is perfectly wise, then we can trust him for his plans in our lives. If we know him to be perfectly loving, then we can believe him even when something doesn't appear to be the product of his love.

That is why in Psalm 31 David, despite the apparent triumph of his enemies, can say, with a strong Hebrew adversative, "*But* I trust in you, O Yahweh." Greatly to the contrary of how we might normally react—in fear, because of who our enemies are—the poet is able to trust Yahweh because of who He is.

The Hebrew verb *to trust* is related to the noun for "security." We trust in Yahweh because he alone is able to give us genuine security. When enemies of every sort are filling our lives with sadness or terror, it is the best of hope to remember that Yahweh is faithful and can be trusted.

In these days of vast unemployment and economic chaos, no one can trust in work or money anymore. Turmoil over personal matters leaves us feeling terribly lonely and insecure. In the midst of doubting and searching, we must continually go back to re-examine the character of Yahweh; again and again the Scriptures assure us that his character can be trusted. Knowing that he loves us with the compassion of a father (Ps. 103:13) or a mother (Isa. 49:13–15) or a shepherd (John 10: 1–3, 11–16), we can find the security for which we long.

That is why the psalmist continues, "I say, 'You are my God.' " The Hebrew verb here could be understood in either of two ways. If it is connected to the adversative *but* that begins the verse, then the verb is an incomplete one and means that the poet is continually saying, "You are my God." Or it could be a perfect (finished-action) verb, meaning that he has said it pointedly, and, therefore, it is a foundation for his life.

In the midst of our struggles, especially when we are lonely, we need to keep reasserting that our God is Yahweh. Otherwise, we fall into the temptation of making idols out of security, or marriage, or companionship, or possessions, or whatever else we think we need to ease our loneliness.

Last Thursday distressing things had been piling up all day long. One of my options for how to use my big house fell through, and I wasn't sure how I'd manage financially. Someone whom I'd been counseling misunderstood my words and got very angry with me without trying to see what I was saying. Then the mail brought me extensive work that I had to do on some writing, and I didn't see how I could fit everything into the schedule. Finally, at about ten that night, I broke down and telephoned a friend for help. My friend wasn't home.

"Now, God, why did you let that happen?"—that was my first reaction. I needed to talk; why, of all times, was there no answer now?

In such disappointment, we need to repeat, "Yahweh, you are my God. I can't rely on human beings to minister to my needs. You are the one to whom I can tell my grief, and you will hear."

Such times remind us that our friends are channels of God's love. Much later that night my friend did call and sort through my troubles with me. But God let me first remember that he alone is God so that I could understand that telephone call as another sign to me of Yahweh's care.

The Hebrew underscores the decisiveness of the psalmist's declaration more than our English translations do. That is why I prefer also to think of the verb *I said* as a decisive, finished action. The Hebrew phrase is literally, "my God—you!" Since pronouns are usually attached to other words in the Hebrew, their appearance as separate entities is always especially emphatic. Also, in this phrase there is no verb, which makes the point even more dramatic: "My God—YOU!" Isn't it a wonder

that we can address him with the second person singular and be
in such a close relationship with him?

If the verb should be decisively rendered "I said" then it
suggests a turning point in the psalmist's life and faith, some
moment at which he realized that God alone is God. Sometimes
we need such a dramatic point at which, reduced to helplessness, we must give up our dependence upon human resources
and say, "my God—YOU!" After we have turned everything
over into his hands, we will become more able to see his love in
action and to feel his comfort in our lives.

Has there been such a major turning point for you? A decisive time when I was a teenager changed the focus and course
of my life profoundly. The God I had known since childhood
became intensely real to me on a stormy night in January. My
wrestling with God matched the wildness of the winter clouds
until I cried from a hospital bed, "My God—YOU!"

But we forget the fact of God's relationship with us at times,
especially in the pain and despair of loneliness and rejection.
When these times come, we must re-sort our priorities and deal
with our doubts in order to come again to the declaration,
"Yes. All other gods cannot be trusted. Everything else will
pass away. My God is you, Yahweh, Covenant God!"

In that declaration we join the psalmist in putting our times
back into His hands. And in such a committing of ourselves
into His care, we finally come to peace.

"In your hand" evokes images of tenderness. I remember a
moment when my friend Tim and I were talking through some
very difficult things. I trembled on the verge of tears, and Tim,
one arm fastened to the blood tubes of his kidney dialysis machine, noticed. Immediately he held out his free hand to me,
and, when I gave him mine, he enfolded it safely in both of his.
The comfort of his touch gave me the courage to continue
wrestling with the problem.

It is not that God takes over our lives and controls everything
arbitrarily. No, rather, in his hands he gives us the perfect freedom to be wholly ourselves, yet under his infinitely wise and
loving care. He lets us choose how to spend our times, but he
will warn us if we go the wrong way (see Isa. 30:21). He will

guide us through our very own desires, which have been made completely new in our faith (see 1 Cor. 5:17).

When we can rest enough to trust with our times the One who is trustable, then we don't have to ask the "how long?" questions. We will be able to see that however long God wants certain processes to continue is simply the gift of his perfect wisdom.

The psalmist goes on to request that God deliver him from his enemies, since his times are in Yahweh's hands. Because the plural noun *times* connotes many experiences and developments, deliverance must not be simplistically understood. We might not be delivered out of the hands of certain enemies. But Yahweh's hand allows us to be transformed, so that the enemy cannot triumph over us. Our times might not be changed, but *we* will be changed in those times. Furthermore, we will become more able to see some of God's purposes in them.

Because I am a free-lancer, my professional life depends upon invitations for speaking engagements. Thoroughly amazing to me has been the way God has filled up my schedule for the past four years. Always there has been plenty of work to do, yet whenever I have needed time to write, there have been appropriate blank spots in my calendar.

Now you might be thinking that it isn't comforting at all to you to see God's hand in my schedule if your own remains empty. I experience also the pain of time that seems to be out of control. In the anguish of long sleepless nights, the darkness of sobs for grief, the confusion of a future that is a vacuum—I confess that it has been impossible for me to trust.

The point is that we are each "on the grow" in learning to trust. We will sometimes fail to trust, because we will always be human. Yet in those times the character of Yahweh is all the more precious to us, because we continually learn afresh that he is a forgiving and affirming God, our Comforter. Therefore, we are set free to go on, feebly trusting, but learning, by means of the Psalms, to trust him more (see especially Chapter 9).

As we are studying passages from the Scriptures together, we are being changed. This is the promise of the word of Yahweh:

It never comes back empty but, like the rain, accomplishes the purposes for which it was sent (see Isa. 55:10–11). Its watering produces the fruit of deeper trusting.

FOR FURTHER MEDITATION

1. Who is Yahweh for me? What is his character?
2. Why can we trust him?
3. At what decisive moment have I said, "My God—YOU!"?
4. What things pull me away from remembering that he is my God?
5. How does it feel to be in the hands of God? Why do I or do I not like that image?
6. How have I experienced God's timing in my life?
7. How do I want to be changed in my times so that I can rest in God's hands, even if the times themselves aren't changed?

3. God Hears My Cries of Panic

In my alarm I said,
"I am cut off from your sight!"
Yet you heard my cry for mercy
when I called to you for help.
Psalm 31:22

Into your hands I commit my spirit;
redeem me, O LORD, the God of truth.
Psalm 31:5

I was ugly, and I knew it. I was a junior in high school, and it
was perfectly clear that I was *the* "class wallflower." Five feet
six inches tall, I was so ill that I weighed only eighty-four
pounds and had no coloring at all. I hated to look in mirrors
because all I saw was a skinny gray pole—hardly a person at all.
I was ugly and unwanted; that was the truth about me.

Undiagnosed illness was the problem, but I was even more
wounded emotionally by my own perception of reality. Consequently, I was excruciatingly lonely.

I wouldn't have had to be lonely. Other girls not very pretty
certainly had friends enough. My own mistaken perception of
the truth inhibited me from reaching out to others, except to
trounce them in academic affairs, and, as a result, the alienation and loneliness grew.

How we perceive the reality of our lives makes all the difference in the world. And that is what the psalmist discusses in
these two disjoint verses from Psalm 31. As you remember
from the last chapter, Psalm 31 speaks about our times being in
God's hands. The whole context of this psalm describes the
poet feeling oppressed by his enemies and needing to claim
Yahweh as his God and the basis for trust. At this point you
might want to reread the entire psalm to put this chapter's
discussion in context.

Just before his closing injunction to all his listeners, the poet
summarizes his troubles. Then, because he remembers how his

God rescued him, he urges us, too, to love Yahweh, to be strong, and to take heart as we hope in him. Since we would like to follow that injunction, we want to pay careful attention to the poet's basis for such an exhortation.

The psalmist remembers that he had spoken out of panic when he said, "I am cut off" (v. 22). His personal dismay is underscored in Hebrew by the addition of the pronoun *I*, which isn't necessary because it is already attached to the verb. Thus, the phrase emphasizes, "I *myself* said in my alarm." "Alarm" comes from the verb meaning "to be in a hurry or trepidation," which here is in the idiomatic form of an infinitive together with the preposition *in*. Thus, the phrase literally says, "I myself said in-my-to-be-in-trepidation." This Hebrew idiom graphically pictures what caused the poet to think he was cut off: a state of panic.

The idiom provides a significant clue for understanding much of our loneliness. Panic affects our perceptions of the truth: We think that we are cut off because, in our panic, that is the only reality we are able to see. However, managing our emotions better might help us to assess the situation more accurately.

Think with me about this healing concept by remembering specific examples in your own experience. Two weekends ago when I was in Minneapolis to speak for a singles conference, a clearer perception of reality gave me powerful assurance. Rereading some materials to prepare for my class on coping with divorce, I struggled again with my feelings of abandonment— even beginning to wonder whether friends would still be there for me when I got back from my work trips. Then I stood up and put on some hand lotion, which had been a birthday present from my friend Tim. I closed my Bible, which was marked by a bookmark that he had given me for that weekend to remind me of his prayers while I spoke. Then I put on my jacket, brightened by a brilliant pink rose appliqued on the pocket. Yes, he had given me that, too. Tim's presents always reminded me of the depth of our friendship, which grew with each of our many long discussions while he was on the kidney machine.

Now I felt immeasurably strengthened for my classes and

assembly speech. I could hardly wait to tell Tim that I knew the
depth of his friendship even when far away. His reminders had
thoroughly registered.

How often we overlook the reminders of God. In our panic,
we might suppose that we are cut off from God, but that is not
the truth of our lives.

The Hebrew original shows much more clearly than our English translations how violent our alarm becomes. In its basic
form the verb that we translate "I am cut off" means "to exter-
minate." It is related to the common noun for "ax," but this is
the only use of the verb in the Old Testament. Such a rare and
violent word emphasizes that the poet's panic caused him to
fear unduly that he had been obliterated from Yahweh's sight,
axed out of his goodness forever.

We don't usually comprehend how violent panic is to us. It
robs us of the truth and causes us to overaccentuate the negative. That is why we say such extreme things as "Nobody helps
me," "Everybody rejects me," or "There isn't anyone who
loves me." Into such emotional extremism, Yahweh wants to
bring the comfort of reality.

In his summary conclusion, the psalmist remembers that God
has ministered to his needs. He further recognizes the great
disparity between his perceptions and the truth of his situation.

The second half of verse 22 begins in the Hebrew text with a
word that the NIV translates "yet." I prefer the translation
"surely," but even that rendering is not strong enough. The
Hebrew particle emphasizes a contrast, especially after verbs
like *I said* or *I thought,* in order to express the reality, in opposition to what had been wrongly imagined. Other translations
could be "but, indeed," or "but, in fact." In other words, after
the psalmist has shown us his dread alarm and how it caused
him to misunderstand terribly, now he will tell us, greatly to
the contrary, what the truth actually was.

The poet proclaims that Yahweh, true to his character, had
"heard my cry for mercy when I called . . .[to him] for help."
The Hebrew text says literally, "You heard the voice of my
supplications," which means "the sound of my distress" or my
"lament" with the "supplications" or "cries" in the plural, as it

is used also in Psalms 28:2, 6; 86:6; and 130:2. Looking at these psalms, too, helps us understand more thoroughly the poet's expression of anguish.

Significantly, some scholars think that the verb we translate "called" is akin to the verb that means "to deliver." That similarity enriches our comprehension of God's answer to our cries. He hears our lament and answers with a deliverance that matches our call.

Because of his strong memory of Yahweh's rescue, the psalmist can conclude with a great exhortation to his readers to love Him and to be strong because of their hope in Him. We will examine that idea in terms of one of the initial verses of the psalm.

When I first spent time thinking about this psalm, almost a year ago, I was struck by the frequency of the word *refuge* in the first five verses. The word connotes a place of safety, a harbor, some sort of protection, and at that time I desperately needed the LORD as a refuge. I was using my home for crisis ministry at that time and had cared for several months for a young runaway who now was complaining about me to the crisis centers and at school because I was trying to help her find a more suitable living situation.

The morning that I studied this psalm in my devotional time, I got an irate phone call condemning me for my treatment of her, and none of the accusations had any basis in truth. Throughout that day I reflected on the comfort of this psalm and tried to assert verse 5 with the psalmist, "Into your hands [Yahweh] I commit my spirit." I wanted Yahweh to be in control of the situation so that I would not react out of a spirit of hurt pride or an eagerness for vindication against my ungrateful houseguest, in whom I had invested a lot of care and money and time and prayer.

As I have studied the psalm more deeply, however, I have learned that the verb *to commit* involves more than an easy dependence arising out of desperation. It occurs here in a causative (Hiphil) form of a word originally meaning "to visit at a muster (of troops)" and, therefore, connotes "to review." Thus, it means more profoundly to give attention to something. When we commit our spirit into Yahweh's hand, our action is carefully intentional, seeking thoroughly to entrust our whole being into his care. It is not a superficial handing over—and we don't take it back!

We can best understand the true nature of thorough committing by realizing at what point Jesus quoted this psalm. Just as he rested his head in death and completed all that had been prophesied about him, he called out, with a victorious cry, "It is finished" (John 19:30), and then, triumphantly, "Father, into your hands I commit my spirit" (Luke 23:46). If God is asking for our total commitment into his hand, then it means death to ourselves (a topic that we will explore further in later chapters).

Because Jesus called out these words at the point of his death, we New Testament believers can more thoroughly understand the assurance of the very next phrase in the psalm: "You have ransomed me, Yahweh." Since Jesus perfectly committed everything into the Father's hand and fulfilled every dimension of His plan, we can be confident that we are indeed ransomed, which means the price has been paid to buy us back from being caught in prisons of sin and death and pain and loneliness.

Most significant to us in our present study, however, is that the poet then calls Yahweh "God of truth." That is exactly what we need to know to be released from those four bondages: the truth about ourselves.

The truth of our relation to sin is that we are forgiven. The truth of our relation to death is that it has been overcome and we do not need to fear it. (See Rev. 2:10–11.) The truth of our relation to pain is that it will never be more than we can bear. And the truth of our loneliness is that when we feel totally cut off, we have in our panic forgotten the reality of God's thorough faithfulness. He is the God of the *amen* (the Hebrew word for truth). Yahweh alone is the God of reliability and stability. And his gift to us in our loneliness is the whole truth about ourselves.

If I had known it then, when I struggled over my ugliness in high school, I would have realized that my appearance was not the whole truth about me. The God of truth had declared his love for me, but I hadn't heard it very well.

The whole truth about us is that we are beloved to Yahweh. We are bought out of our enslavement to any lack of self-es-

teem. Rather, the truth, as Jesus says, sets us free (John 8:32).
He further promises that as we continue to study his word we
will know the truth—and we shall be free indeed (John 8:31,
36).

FOR FURTHER MEDITATION

1. How have I observed that my alarm prevents me from accurately assessing my situation?
2. What misjudgments have made me feel cut off from Yahweh's sight and love?
3. How have I been enabled to discover that such perception was not the whole reality?
4. How has Yahweh delivered me when I cried to him for help?
5. Am I able thoroughly to commit my spirit into Yahweh's hands? Why or why not?
6. How does Christ's work to buy me back from prisons of pain and death affect my understanding of God's action in other dimensions of my life?
7. How does the truth about me set me free?

4. My Trust Won't Put Me to Shame

To you, O LORD, I lift up my soul;
  in you I trust, O my God.
Do not let me be put to shame,
  nor let my enemies triumph over me.
Psalm 25:1–2

Immediately my head was raised as if by a pulley—an automatic reaction to the sermon I had heard in chapel just a few days before. A favorite professor had commented on the Joy of this pastoral invitation and congregational refrain from the Lutheran liturgy: "Lift up your hearts." "We lift them up unto the Lord." The privilege of that invitation has all too often lost its impact, especially for those who have been singing those words since childhood.

The wondrous privilege of going to God with our desires and thanksgivings makes a shamefaced looking at the floor out of place. The pastor's challenge ought also to be, "Lift up your heads." The Scriptures constantly invite us to lift up our heads or hearts or souls or eyes in order to observe the character of our God and to see his action on our behalf.

As we continue in this chapter to lay the basis for understanding how God wants to comfort us in our times of loneliness, we pause to be intentional about lifting up our souls to Yahweh. The Hebrew text of this first verse of Psalm 25 begins with the phrase, "Unto you, Yahweh." Putting this first underscores the direction. Toward Yahweh we want to be devoting our attention and desire in the course of everyday life.

A few weeks ago I waited in the hall of the kidney center in Seattle while Tim went through a dialysis run. I could choose my direction—to focus on my discomfort or the privilege. To have waited miserably—hearing the agony of those patients who were having hard runs and wishing that I could be home in my soft bed—would have prohibited the learning.

But to try to help some of the patients as they finished runs or to minister to relatives and friends who waited stirred up great gratitude for my healthy kidneys and for the dialysis that keeps my friend alive. The intricacies of God's creation and the graciousness of his protection made me long for my life to be more characterized by this direction: "Unto you, Yahweh."

In the second phrase of the psalm the poet lifts up to Yahweh his soul. Sunday school lessons from childhood convinced me that the soul was some little, bitty part of me that went to heaven when I died and my body went into the ground. The Hebrew concept, used frequently in the Psalms, is much larger than that.

The word *nephesh,* first of all, means the living being, as in Genesis 2:7, which declares that God breathed into man and he became a living being. Derived from that first meaning is the definition "the true self, the essential part of a person." From that meaning, *nephesh* has come to signify the seat of one's emotions and passions, one's mental acts—even the will.

The last definition—the will—seems most appropriate here in Psalm 25. We need to lift up to Yahweh intentionally the true core of ourselves, our will and desires. This understanding is further confirmed as appropriate when we compare this verse to Psalm 24:4, where the liturgist at the temple declares that the one who may ascend the hill of the LORD is the one "who has clean hands and a pure heart [both outside and inside purity], who does not lift up his soul to an idol. . . ." Instead, "Unto you, Yahweh," we lift up our souls.

The fact that the soul includes our will helps us specifically in times of loneliness. When we feel abandoned because God is not there, we can still by an act of will lift up our minds to him. We do not have to exert frantic energies to secure God's attention or forgiveness, but we can focus on him with intentionality to receive more readily his comforting answers to our cries.

The verb is a continuing one, "I am lifting up." To direct our desires to Yahweh can't be done just once, decisively, for all time. Rather, the constant discipline of our daily lives must be to keep ourselves pointed toward Yahweh. So many things in the world distract us, so many negative attitudes in our faith draw us away from him, so many griefs in our days make us cry out against him. No matter what is happening in our lives, the psalmist invites us to be lifting up our souls to Yahweh.

An important goal for our spiritual growth is to become so directed toward the LORD that every situation is immediately turned over to him. If we could learn instantly to refer whatever happens to his wisdom and guidance, we could faithfully practice his presence in every moment of our lives.

To help that to develop, we can establish daily disciplines of prayer and Bible study and meditation. The more thoroughly we enfold ourselves in God's presence in our devotional times, the more readily he will be apparent to us in the other moments of the day.

The second verse of this psalm doubly emphasizes the relationship with God. Not only does it contain the phrase "in you," but also God is addressed as the object of trust and called "my God." In the Hebrew text the phrase "my God" is in an emphatic position, so that the relationship takes first importance. This stresses that we trust not in an unreachable God far away and transcendent, but he is "*my* God," the one who personally cares for me and for you and has chosen us for himself. The constant message of the Scriptures is that God wants to relate to us. As a bumper sticker quips, "If we're not feeling close to God, guess who moved." Surely, he will remain our God, even more than we could ever want him to be.

Furthermore, in the Hebrew text *trusted* is in the perfect tense here, signifying finished action. That means that the act of trusting in God was a point of commitment that has been decisive. Now, its results still stand. In realizing that to Yahweh we want to lift up our souls, our direction in all circumstances has been established.

This intentionality has significant implications for the way in which we read the Scriptures. We can choose to read them as Law or as Gospel, as our objectives for the day, which we *must* reach, or as our goals for the direction of our lives, the way in which we are *learning* to move.

If we read exhortations, such as to "put on compassion," as Law, we are crushed by our failure, for it is impossible for us thoroughly to put on compassion. If we see those same exhortations as Gospel invitations, then to be compassionate is our goal; it orients the direction in which we move through our days, but it is not the day's objective, which we will have failed to meet if we don't get there by tonight. Our day's objectives might be to do *acts* of compassion, like caring for a sick neighbor or giving more money away to help the poor, but these are simply movements toward the goal of being a thoroughly compassionate person.

When we first believed in Christ by his invitation, we set our goal, in response to his love: to imitate his obedient life. In each day we experience many moments characterized by his life in us, though we also often fail. But our direction has been set. In the course of living it out, more and more we want to choose faithfully to lift up our souls to him.

This contrast is the same in Paul's words about putting off the old, sinful nature and putting on the new and about being renewed daily by the Spirit's work in our minds and lives (see Eph. 4:22–24). The first two are decisive actions (according to the tense used in Greek), the once-and-for-all setting free of God's justification. The third is the constant process of renewal, the sanctification that is our daily lifting up of the soul to Yahweh. The two go hand in hand in the Scriptures, but we must always understand the difference, lest we become overwhelmed by a burden that instead should set us free.

The poet's last two phrases are powerful arguments in his pleas to God. "Do not let me be put to shame" assumes that the enemies are watching to see if his faith is grounded in reality. Moses makes the same sort of plea when he says to God, in essence, "Don't destroy Israel now. Then what would those say who wondered about your taking us out of Egypt? They will think, 'Did he take them out just to kill them?' " (Exod. 32:11–14). Ultimately, for us to be shamed reflects back on the character of our God.

Though that might seem like blackmailing God, really we are invited by him so to understand our relationship with him. For us to be put to shame would mean that God cannot be trusted. Because he has demonstrated throughout history that he is thoroughly faithful, we can be sure he will never let that happen.

We must be careful, in our loneliness, not to misunderstand

such a concept. A lonely woman cannot say, "God, you must give me a husband. If you don't, I will be put to shame since I have told others that you grant prayer requests." I am bothered by some of the theology going around these days—that we can "claim" God's action in our lives for certain material requests. Some pray, "Lord, we claim your healing" or "Lord, I claim that you have a wife for me." How can those who pray in this way be so sure that they understand God's perfect will?

We won't ever be put to shame for our trusting in God, but perhaps we each have felt shamed when our trust has been in our own visions for how God should work things out. Faithfully to lift up our souls to Yahweh and to trust in him means to believe him for the ways in which he will guarantee that we will not be shamed.

The last phrase, "nor let my enemies triumph over me," reminds us that we do all have enemies, which are constantly changing. The question is not whether or not we will have them, but whether or not they will triumph over us. Our enemies can be our fears or doubts, people, circumstances, illness, confusion. If we are constantly lifting up our souls to Yahweh to find his presence in the midst of these oppressions, they cannot be victorious over us.

Such is very much the case with this oppressive loneliness against which I often struggle. Whenever I turn in it to the comfort of the Psalms and the hope of Yahweh's guidance, that loneliness cannot destroy me. When I let it have its way by neglecting my devotional disciplines or failing to believe that God is present, then the loneliness seems to overwhelm me.

God doesn't want these enemies to triumph over us. He made the victory sure in the death of his Son. What remains is for us to be more intentional about turning to him so that he can apply that victory to the particular battles of our own human lives.

FOR FURTHER MEDITATION

1. How intentional is the lifting up of my soul?
2. What improvements would I like to make in my personal devotional habits?

3. How can I learn to exert my will over my emotions—choosing to trust God even when I don't feel like it?
4. How do I know that Yahweh is MY God, even when he doesn't seem to be?
5. How do I understand the difference between justification and sanctification, the once-and-for-all trusting in Yahweh and the daily turning of my soul to him?
6. How have I seen that I am ashamed because of my own failures rather than that God allows me to be shamed?
7. How have I let enemies triumph over me when I didn't need to? How does the victory of Christ over evil become more thoroughly a part of my daily life?

5. God's Mother-Love

Remember, O LORD, your great mercy and love,
  for they are from of old.
Remember not the sins of my youth
  and my rebellious ways;
according to your love remember me,
  for you are good, O LORD. . . .
All the ways of the LORD are loving and faithful
  for those who keep the demands of his covenant.

Psalm 25:6–7, 10

My back porch on that miserable summer afternoon was sti-fling and empty. I had just had a fight with my best friend and, in my fierce anger, had told her that if she didn't want to do things my way, she could just go home. So she did.

I was about ten and the loneliest I'd ever been. Finally my despair overcame even my pride, and I raced to her house on the other side of our church to ask her forgiveness and seek reconciliation. I couldn't stand being without her. I knew all too well that my own sin had alienated her.

Similarly, plain old sin frequently causes our adult loneliness. Alienated from God and from the people around us because of our pride or temper or stupidities, we grapple with the sin and guilt that isolate us. The pattern of Psalm 25 is instructive for our removing those obstructions so that relationships might be restored.

Verses 6 and 7 are structured chiastically in Hebrew. That means that "remember," which appears in verse 6, appears at the end of the initial phrase of verse 7; then the objects of those verbs both appear in the middle between them. Thus, the phrases read literally as follows:

Remember your compassions, Yahweh. And your loving-kindnesses
  for from long duration they (are).
The sins of my youth and my transgressions do not remember.

The emphasis of "remember" and "do not remember" gives us hope in the face of sin. When we address God as Yahweh, this special covenant name emphasizes that he will *for sure* remember his compassions. This is the character asserted in the name, "I AM."

If he does not remember, he has, out of the fullness of his love, deliberately set something aside. The nature of God's forgiveness, the Old Testament frequently assures us, is that when he sets sins aside, he remembers them no more (see, for example, Jer. 31:34).

Instead, the psalmist asks Yahweh to remember his "compassions." The Hebrew term comes from the noun meaning "womb" and therefore implies the mother-love of God. When her baby cries, a mother can't resist picking the child up to comfort it and meet its needs. In the same way, we are baby-helpless before God. This is one of many Old Testament passages that remind us that the image of God is both male and female. In his/her womb-compassions, his/her infinite mother-love, Yahweh answers our cries.

The psalmist is holding God to the character that he has revealed over the ages. With an idiom used frequently in the Old Testament, David reminds Yahweh that his loving-kindnesses (a plural term, as is *compassions*) have been from ancient times. Truly, if Yahweh has demonstrated his kindness in manifest displays of caring for Israel throughout its turbulent history, then God's character could hardly change now. Knowing that Yahweh will remember, the poet can turn with confidence from his sin and hope with assurance for forgiveness.

The poet further asks Yahweh to turn away from remembering those sins. The two words that he chooses for evil acts create a glaring contrast to the two terms that were the objects of Yahweh's remembering. The first word, which we translate "sin," comes from the verb meaning "to miss a goal or way, to go wrong," as when a person aims for the target, but the arrow flies off into the field. Our lives are characterized by such missing of God's marks, because often we aim wrong and sometimes we slip as we shoot. Whatever the reason we miss the target, our alienation from God produces loneliness.

We each recognize how our own selfishness causes us to miss

the mark. When I am with someone who is very comforting to me, I sometimes catch myself soaking up gifts with no thought at all of caring for the other's needs. Intense loneliness can come when the bond between us is marred by my concern only for myself.

The second word, which the NIV translates "rebellious ways," is often rendered "transgressions." The term implies a deliberate defiance, the choice to step across the line. Much of the alienation of our times comes because the so-called freedom to violate God's plans for physical affection has made everyone unsure of true intimacy. If, for example, a girl chooses to indulge in sex outside of marriage and without the commitment that God intends to be the foundation for that gift, she will often experience the crushing loneliness of nagging doubts about whether or not her partner really loves her.

The poet asks that Yahweh not deal with him on the basis of these many sins of omission and commission, the slipping and the rebellion. If God were to relate to us on that basis, there would be no hope whatsoever.

The good news of the gospel, in contrast, is that God has chosen instead to act toward us according to his *chesedh*, his loving-kindness, as seen especially in redemption from sin. Not according to our character, but according to his character of steadfast love and faithfulness, God will remember us.

Once again a poetic duplication underscores the good news. The psalmist adds a parallel phrase, which says literally in the Hebrew, "for the sake of your goodness, Yahweh." The word *for-the-sake-of* reminds us that God will maintain his character. As the Apostle Paul writes in 2 Timothy 2:13, the LORD "cannot disown himself." His character is to be good, so that, no matter how un-good his people are, he will act that way toward them, instead of reacting to their sinful rebellion and tragic failure to hit the target.

God's goodness is infinite, not only in its extent, but also in the myriads of ways that it is manifested. Most of the Psalms record dimensions of God's goodness as they recount such things as his actions toward his people (see, for example, Psalm 105), the wonders of his creation (Psalm 104), and his constancy in forgiveness (Psalm 103).

In the psalm before us, the poet tells us three verses later that all the ways of Yahweh are characterized by steadfast love and fidelity. The last word of this pair is related to the word *amen* and emphasizes the truth that Yahweh always acts according to his attributes. His reliable faithfulness can always be trusted.

Many years ago a woman who had returned from Peace Corps service in the Pacific islands was having a terrible time re-adjusting to the United States. She struggled with severe depression and, within it, an intense loneliness. As we studied the Scriptures together weekly, she began to practice the habit of repeating, when she felt overcome by waves of despair, the simple phrase, "*God* is faithful. God *is* faithful. God is *faithful!*"

With great Joy one day she brought me a present of a new box of tissues, decorated with a bow. Asked what we were celebrating, she replied, "Last weekend God and I conquered a downer all by myself." In the midst of her repetition of the fact that God is faithful, its meaning had finally sunk in, and she recognized his presence with her in that pain.

An amusing addendum to her story occurred several months later when I was very discouraged about moving and finding my place in a new situation. Her gentle reminder, "Marva, don't forget: God is faithful," stimulated a necessary change of attitude for me.

The second part of verse 10 illustrates the importance of reading the Scriptures in their context; the addition of "for those who keep the demands of his covenant" seems to qualify God's faithfulness, as if it were available only to those who were perfectly obedient. Such a requirement might drive us to despair and intensify our loneliness.

Notice, instead, the place of verse 10 in this context:

Verse 8: Good and upright is the LORD;
          therefore he instructs sinners in his ways.

(This verse stresses the connection between the character of Yahweh and the availability of his instruction.)

Verse 9: He guides the humble in what is right
          and teaches them his way.

(Once again we are reminded that we learn to obey by Yahweh's gracious instruction.)

> Verse 10: All the ways of the LORD are loving and faithful
> for those who keep the demands of his covenant.
> Verse 11: For the sake of your name, O LORD,
> forgive my iniquity, though it is great.

After we have been reminded that our ability to "keep the demands of his covenant" has been taught us by Yahweh's guidance, we are also immediately reminded that in our great failures we are forgiven. No matter how deliberate our trespassing or how widely we miss the mark, because Yahweh is true to his character—that is, for the sake of his name—we can trust in his forgiveness.

My sin against my childhood playmate had been great. Not because I was so good at repenting, but because it was in her character, she readily assented to my tearful plea for forgiveness. My loneliness vanished in her grace.

Similarly, when we receive the forgiveness for our sin that Yahweh holds out to us, many kinds of loneliness are dispelled. We can return from our alienation and find Joy in the LORD's presence. Furthermore, that restoration often gives us the freedom and courage to pursue restorations with others, as we will consider in later chapters. Because the ways of Yahweh are loving and faithful, we respond by keeping the demands of his covenant.

FOR FURTHER MEDITATION

1. Have I mistrusted God by acting as if in his infinite nature he could not deliberately *not* remember?
2. What images does the concept of the mother-love of God create for me?
3. How does the constancy of God's faithfulness over the ages give me courage for today?
4. How have I experienced God's forgiveness for all the sins of my youth? and my adulthood?
5. How have I seen that God must be true to his character? What is "the sake of" his name?

6. Is even God's venting of wrath a dimension of his loving-kindness? How?

7. How can I be set free from the worry that my inability to keep his covenant demands will prevent me from experiencing that all his ways are loving and faithful?

6. Lonely and Afflicted—But Yahweh Releases Me from the Snare

My eyes are ever on the LORD
for only he will release my feet from the snare.
Turn to me and be gracious to me,
for I am lonely and afflicted.
The troubles of my heart have multiplied;
free me from my anguish.
Look upon my affliction and my distress
and take away all my sins.

Psalm 25:15–18

This morning I went to the pool feeling troubled at having been misunderstood in my ministry. I found it harder than usual to move past the first painful laps of my workout. However, I have been using that swimming time to meditate on the Psalms, and, as favorite passages floated around in my brain, my floating in the water became easier. Tension drained from my body as God's promises brought me their deep comfort. His love, in which I felt enfolded, set my mind free to think more clearly. By the time I got to Psalm 30 and spoke the words, "Weeping may remain for a night, but rejoicing comes in the morning," I felt exultant in the actual experience of that transformation.

The first line of the psalm section we are considering here challenges each of us to deepen our devotional lives. When the poet says, literally, "my eyes continually to Yahweh," he invites us to develop habits of practicing God's presence in every situation. Such habits are best rooted in specific disciplined times of Bible study and meditation and prayer.

Perhaps you need, as I do, the encouragement of this psalmist who seems to be diligent in devotional disciplines. I get angry with myself because I know that I would not struggle

against loneliness and frustration and grief as much as I do if
my eyes were more frequently fixed on Yahweh.

The NIV translation of "for only he will release my feet from
the snare," retains the emphasis in the Hebrew text. The addition of the separate pronoun *he* to the *he* already included in
the verb stresses uniqueness: "he indeed" or "only he" or
"truly he." That thrust urges us to observe more carefully how
often we try to get our feet out of the net by our own strength
or wisdom, our own devices and strategems.

The case this morning is a good example. I thought I was
snared by someone else's misunderstanding, but actually I was
ensnared by my own pride. Much of my anguish centered on
my own need to clarify things.

When you've been the target of misunderstanding or false
rumors, how much of your anguish has centered on your own
need to clarify? If the LORD alone is the one who can get us out
of our snares, then we need to fix our eyes on him in order to
learn how he wants to do it. My meditation in the pool today
brought astonishing results.

The first several psalms, especially the nineteenth, encourage
greater openness to God's instruction. Then Psalm 22, which
begins with the agonizing question, "My God, my God, why
have you forsaken me?" brought into my mind other things
that Jesus said when taking our place in death. Thinking about
him saying also from the cross, "Father, forgive them, for they
do not know what they are doing" (Luke 23:34), I realized that
was true also for anyone who speaks falsely about us. We are
misunderstood because others are too much burdened by their
own pain. God's method for bringing us out of the snare is not
for us to correct the rumors and set everybody straight, but for
us to swallow our pride, forgive the ones who malign us, and
seek somehow to ease their pain.

What sorts of snares have entrapped your feet? How can
looking eagerly and consistently to Yahweh bring you out of
those traps? Whether others have spread the nets against us or
we have tangled up ourselves, Yahweh alone is the one who can
bring us out successfully.

The overwhelming good news about God is that he really
wants to release us. Sometimes I think that if I were he, I would
just leave me in some of the messes I cook up for myself. But

when the poet goes on to say, "Turn to me and be gracious to me," the word *turn* strikes us with its royal reaching out.

The Hebrew word means "to regard," in the sense of either caring about someone or fixing one's attention on something. Considering all our mistakes and rebellions, what right do we have to expect that God would turn to look at us? Yet he always deigns to do so; our asking reminds us that he does.

Why does a parent respond by looking when a little child calls out, "Watch me"? Usually the child is not doing anything extraordinary. Rather, the love of a father or mother makes room for spending time to encourage the child. In the same way the father/mother-love of God chooses to watch us in grace.

The poet continues by lamenting his loneliness as a time with a special need for someone to watch with love. Don't you sometimes feel that what you need more than anything is for someone to care about the little things in your life?

This concept of God's gracious regarding is especially comforting if we have lived for any length of time in a situation in which we were not accepted—when the heart of someone around us has been closed to us, so that nothing that we do could ever meet with approval. When we know that we have lost even before starting, we struggle to crank up the energy to try. How we are released when we find friends who like what we do, who approve of us unconditionally, so that in their grace we have the freedom to do better!

The freedom with which the psalmist can say, "Turn to me and be gracious to me," comes from knowing that God, who has received him lovingly in the past, cannot be false to his character of covenant faithfulness. Therefore, we can with bold confidence—made more sure in the manifestation of God's love in the person of Jesus—go immediately to God and ask for his attention (see Eph. 3:12).

"For I am lonely and afflicted," the poet despairs. The more poignant Hebrew phrase says, literally, "for solitary and afflicted—I." The word for "solitary" means "the only one," an isolated individual who is friendless and a wanderer, a lonely exile. That forsakenness is often matched in the Old Testament with weakness, poverty, or other needy affliction. Note also that this is another phrase that concludes with an emphatic pronoun *I* and no verb. Both devices accentuate the starkness of this state of being: to be without any human comforter in the midst of affliction.

Such statements help us remember that we are not the only ones who suffer the pain of loneliness. But even that might not be much of a comfort if it is for us an unremitting fact of life.

There is, however, another fact in our existence. The poet has been reminding us, as we despair over the lack of human comfort, that God is present with steady faithfulness to look upon us with love. We don't have to feel this fact. Indeed, sometimes in acknowledging it as a fact we might begin to feel his presence as well. Even if we don't feel it, truly God's tender regarding does enfold us.

Even when the poet's troubles are multiplied, as he declares in the next phrase, he knows that God is able to free him from that anguish. Looking closely at his complaint might help us to better understand some of our own despair. When he says, literally, "the distresses of my heart have been enlarged," the phrase uses graphically descriptive words that ring true to our experience in an age of tension and stress. The word I translated "distresses" comes from the verb meaning "to bind, tie up, or be restricted or cramped." It is related to the word for "tight" or "narrow." Sometimes we feel that the world's troubles are hemming us in so tightly that we can't breathe.

Again, we are reminded that only Yahweh can bring us out of the snare, for the poet turns to him to "free me from my anguish." Free is the same word as *release* in the snare phrase in verse 15. *Anguish* is more particular than the word I translated "distresses" in connoting constraints in the sense of pressures and stress.

Especially in these days of economic pressures and widespread unemployment, we learn that only Yahweh can bring us out. Many of my friends who are searching for work and for some sort of security are realizing that whatever the world offers can never be sure. As the pressures mount, the only place to find true release from their straits is in the comfort of knowing personally the gracious Lord who chooses to look upon us with care.

That is why the poet then appeals again to Yahweh's tender concern for his affliction and distress. This time, however, he acknowledges another fact: By asking God to take away all his sins, he seems to imply that those same sins are the root cause of his troubles. If God will remove the source, then the poet can be freed from those symptoms of his sin.

We need to recognize continually the significant part sin plays in our distresses, but not in order to overwhelm us with guilt about our inability to be the persons we want to be. Rather, when we have a deep enough sense of our sin, we will be more ready to receive the forgiveness that God freely offers. When we begin to have a more profound sense of that gracious forgiveness, we will become more able to accept ourselves. Finally, when we can accept ourselves more, we will be set free to think more clearly and to deal more decisively with our afflictions and distresses. Only when we are enfolded in love do we have the power to find hope.

The psalm ends with a plea for protection and a final declaration that the poet's hope is in Yahweh. That takes us back full circle to where we began—with the recognition that we need to learn to fix our eyes upon the LORD in order to recognize his presence and the fullness of his care in our lives. Our covenant God is turning to us to be gracious, to release us from the snares, to free us from anguish, to take away our sins. Our loneliness gets lost in the wonder of his comforting care.

FOR FURTHER MEDITATION

1. How effective are my devotional habits for fixing my eyes on the LORD?
2. In what ways do I want to improve them?
3. How have I seen that God's plans were better than mine for bringing my feet out of the snare?
4. How have I experienced the difference between persons looking upon me with grace, and with disapproval?
5. How does the look of grace ease my loneliness?
6. How do I experience distresses ("straightness") in my life?
7. In what ways are my sins the root cause of my distresses and what can I do about that? (Be sure here not to come up with an answer of working yourself out of it. What is the answer of grace?)

7. Yahweh Understands Even Betrayal

I said, "Oh, that I had the wings of a dove!
  I would fly away and be at rest—
I would flee far away
  and stay in the desert;   *Selah*
I would hurry to my place of shelter,
  far from the tempest and storm." . . .
If an enemy were insulting me,
  I could endure it;
if a foe were raising himself against me,
  I could hide from him.
But it is you, a man like myself,
  my companion, my close friend,
with whom I once enjoyed sweet fellowship
  as we walked with the throng at the house of God.
                    Psalm 55:6–8, 12–14

At times I want to run so far away that no one will ever find me. Sometimes I feel so bad that I would give anything simply to drop out of existence. The psalmist David longed, as we do, to escape.

We don't have to feel guilty about wanting to run away from everything or everyone. Psalm 55 shows us legitimate reasons for wanting to give up. What matters is how we deal with this feeling; to be realistic about it is a constructive beginning.

The poet David says, literally, "Who will give to me wings like a dove that I might fly away and settle down to rest?" His longing is born out of a terrible life situation. Several verses later, he says, "Oh, that I had wings to fly away . . . because I see violence and strife in the city. Day and night they prowl about on its walls; malice and abuse are within it. Destructive forces are at work in the city; threats and lies never leave its streets." He is surrounded by all kinds of troubles that are out of his control.

The same is true for us. We live in an age of nuclear madness, of demonic oppression, of violent struggle in the streets, of grinding poverty and escalating crime and mind-damaging drugs and soul-damaging rejection.

There is a place for righteous recoil. We can become so overwhelmed by the pain around us that it seems impossible to go on. At those times our longing for retreat is prompted by a holy restlessness.

The freedom to see it that way comes from a closer look at the night Jesus spent in the Garden of Gethsemane. We can't even begin to comprehend the anguish that he felt as he contemplated the hours ahead. What must he have been feeling as he faced separation from the Father, the very source of his guidance and comfort and strength? What would it be like to be separated from your very self?—indeed, he and the Father are one more closely than we could ever understand.

Nor can we begin to comprehend the intense pain of bearing our sins. We know the guilt that we feel when we do something wrong. How could one ever stand the agony of that enormous weight multiplied by the number of sins in one person's lifetime *times* all the people who have ever lived or will live?

We dare not make it too simple for Jesus. He was God, of course, but he had laid the powers of his God nature aside in order to live and die as a man for us. Consequently, he faced all that physical pain and emotional anguish and spiritual separation with the fears and despair of a human being. Yet, the writer to the Hebrews says, he did not sin (Heb. 4:15).

To be discouraged by the immensity of the tasks or suffering before us is not to sin. What matters is what we do with that frustration or sadness. If we are feeling overwhelmed by the pain of our lives and pray, "Father, if it is possible, remove this cup from me" or "Give me wings to fly away and escape it," we have not sinned. What causes separation from God is our inability to add, "Nevertheless, not what I will, but what you will" (see Matt. 26:36–44).

Are we willing in the midst of everything to believe that God knows best? Do we trust him that if he doesn't fly us away from whatever brings us despair, his plan is, according to his infinite wisdom, best?

Next, the poet reiterates that his purpose was to fly away to rest. He wanted to abide in the desert to be sheltered far away from the storm and tempest.

Solitude is critical for balance. Jesus often retreated from the crowds and the pain of the world around him. He escaped into the hills to pray, to spend time in quiet communion with his Father. It is right for us to get away for times of recuperation and strengthening in order that we might have the will to continue battling the evils against which we are struggling.

We need in our Christianity a better theology of rest. We are often so eager to serve the LORD and to tell others about him that we forget to balance our work with relaxation. Somehow we have neglected the importance of the Old Testament Sabbath in our New Testament faith. The Jews worked hard for six days and rested on the seventh. They recognized the rhythms of life; they realized that we need space to be restored, to rest, to find healing.

In a time of deep depression I had trouble giving myself enough space to work on emotional healing. The Church would be much more relevant in contemporary society if we could learn to help others take enough time for psychological restoration or physical recharging.

That is the value for me of such things as working out in the swimming pool every day, taking time in the midst of my work to play the piano, spending time with friends with whom I can share my struggles and find active support in a listening ear and comforting words. There is a place for fishing trips or hikes in the woods to soak up the warmth of the sunshine and the splendor of God's magnificent creation. There is healing in a hot cup of tea and classical music, a fire in the fireplace and a rocking chair. Whatever gives us strength provides a personally suitable escape so that we can find courage for the tasks ahead.

In fact, the very liturgy of our worship allows time for reflection and soaking up strength. At several points in Psalm 55 the word *selah* appears. I think that *selah* was the first word I ever learned to read. Following my mother's finger in the hymnbook when the Psalms were read responsively in worship, I kept hearing two strange syllables that made no sense to me. I rejoiced to be able to participate in the readings by shouting out "Selah!" at the appropriate places.

The word is thought by most scholars to be some sort of musical directive. Perhaps it noted a pause in the reciting of the psalm during which instruments were played to give participants in the worship service some free time for pondering the words that had just been said.

If this is so, then its placement between verses 7 and 8 is strategic. Having heard the wish of the poet to have wings to fly away to the desert to rest, the worshiper could think about the desirability of rest and its effectiveness. Then the poetry continues with the further wish that such an escape would provide a shelter from the storm and tempest, which are described in the next three verses.

However, after he describes all the violence and destruction that he observes in the world around him, the poet declares that the enemy isn't what is really causing him the most trouble. If it were just an enemy, he could endure it or hide.

We often think in such a manner when we can't cope. If only this weren't the trouble, we muse, we could handle it. Wouldn't it be good, we think, if we could choose our struggles?

The poet continues by describing what for many of us has also been the greatest agony of our aloneness: that it was a close friend who hurt us most deeply. We had "once enjoyed sweet fellowship . . . at the house of God."

The day that I first read this psalm in my morning quiet time, I sat at my desk and wept, because the poem seemed to have been written just for me. So often I have thought that I could handle whatever comes from an enemy, but how can I endure the pain of being betrayed by a friend?

Many of us have searched in vain for an answer to that pain. We'll never find an explanation for the evil that causes those we love to hurt us. Yet the reality of that pain is too overwhelmingly real. "It is you," the poet says, literally, "a man like my row," (sitting in the same row), or "similar to me." In other words, "you are an individual, a human being of my valuation, an equal." Not only that, but you are "my friend and my acquaintance."

Our English words don't reveal the poignancy of these Hebrew expressions. The first word for "friend" implies an intimacy often used to describe the relationship of a woman and her husband. The deep closeness that once existed with the

beloved has been violated. The second comes from a verb that
means "to know" and involves the idea of revealing or discovering. This friend is one to whom the poet has revealed his
innermost self, the deepest truths of his being. Yet this is the
one who has attacked him, who has violated the covenant that
existed between them (see vv. 20–21 of the psalm).

I was profoundly comforted not long ago when I confided to
one of my best friends some of my inmost private feelings
about my life and work and was not laughed at. Months before,
I had revealed those bits of the deepest me to someone else,
who had cast it all off as preposterous. I had wondered then if I
could ever again trust anyone enough to share what really matters in my life.

The poet grieves that once he had enjoyed sweet fellowship
with this close friend. In fact, they had walked together with
the throng of worshipers at the house of God.

Similarly, some of us have known the anguish of betrayal, the
life-ripping, heartbreaking, soul-wrenching despair of having
one that we deeply trusted destroy our lives. A spouse leaves us
for someone else, who was a good friend. A work colleague
maligns our efforts and dirties our reputation. There seems to
be no way to ease that pain. We may have forgiven the one who
hurt us. The fracturing of our lives might have taken place
long ago. Yet we still have occasional nightmares and frequent
flashbacks to bad memories, even as we try to run away from
those scenes. How do we deal with the rending torment that
our lives have been broken apart by someone with whom we
once worshiped?

Perhaps one of the deepest tragedies of sin in the world is
that it hits us in the hardest places. We could expect that the
last source of pain would be the Church. Yet often there we are
most deeply wounded. It might have been the betrayal of some
Christian friend or a spouse. Sometimes it is the policies of a
congregation that have been destructive to us. Many times we
who are single and alone and struggling with our loneliness
have been painfully rejected by those who are supposed to be
the people of God.

I guess this is a point at which I cannot be a theologian anymore. I have no simple answer for the problem of pain. I do

not understand sin. I cannot comprehend the breaking of a marriage vow or deception or adultery or broken commitments. I am not able to cope with the seeming endlessness of grief.

I can't be superficial here. Some of you who read this are suffering terrible anguish right now because of betrayal by Christian people. How can we bear the incomprehensible hurts?

That is the poet's agony. That is ours. And that was the burden of Jesus. Only in that last fact can we begin to find a way to deal with the immensity of the pain.

Jesus endured everything that we do, including betrayal by one of his best friends, so that he knows (see Heb. 4:14). Indeed, he can stand beside us in every aspect of our loneliness and understand. The next chapter will deal with the poet's answers, and then, as we study Psalm 56, we will see even more clearly how much God understands our woe and cares for us in the midst of it.

FOR FURTHER MEDITATION

1. What kinds of experiences make me want to escape?
2. How does it help me to know that Jesus felt like that, too?
3. What sorts of things give me rest so that I can be strengthened?
4. What opportunities for "Selah" meditation does the worship service at my church offer?
5. What kinds of enemies *can* I handle?
6. How have I been deeply hurt by close friends? Have I forgiven them?
7. Have I been deeply hurt in my church? Have I been able to forgive?

8. Evening, Morning, and Noon, He Hears My Voice

> But I call to God,
>   and the LORD saves me.
> Evening, morning and noon
>   I cry out in distress,
>   and he hears my voice. . . .
> Cast your cares on the LORD
>   and he will sustain you;
>   he will never let the righteous fall.
> *Psalm 55:16–17, 22*

The advertisement for Wind Song perfume pictures a young man wistfully imagining a lovely young girl, whose dancing image floats across his head. The caption promises, "He can't get you out of his mind."

That caption serves as a lovely, contemporary paraphrase of the well-known verses, "Cast all your care upon Him, for He careth for you" (1 Pet. 5:7, KJV) and "Cast your cares on the LORD and he will sustain you" (Psalm 55:22). Indeed, God cannot get us out of his mind—not that he would want to, which is the incredible part about it. He would never want to cease caring for us.

As in many other lament psalms, the composer David moves in Psalm 55 from stating his difficulties to asserting "But I call to God." This is the response to adversity by the person of faith. As we continue to study the Psalms together, I pray that more and more this will be our natural response. The more I meditate on the Psalms, the more easily I move into prayer in my daily life. This habit of practicing the presence of God will be our best weapon to combat loneliness in our lives.

When the psalmist continues with the assurance "and the LORD saves me," he uses a Hebrew verb that is a favorite of mine. Most commonly translated "to save" or "to deliver," it actually means "to give width and breadth to" or "to liberate." Since we considered earlier the tightening around him that the poet was experiencing, this image sets up a radical contrast. When the evils around us seem to hem us in more and more closely, the liberation of Yahweh is a glorious giving of space— width and breadth to breathe and move.

Verse 17 forms the focus for our consideration here in this chapter. We must understand it thoroughly to fight a common misconception that is promoted in some prayer groups and that, I'm afraid, is destructive to our relationship with God.

The poet says, literally, "In the evening and in the morning and at middays I will complain and murmur." The word *murmur* creates the image of a soul in dire distress and prayer, to underscore the deep compassion and sympathy with which Yahweh responds. Though the first verb could be translated "to muse," I think that here it should more appropriately be rendered, "to complain." The NIV rendition, "I cry out in distress," doesn't seem to carry the intensity of the Hebrew expression. The poet is roaring with deep pain. He is complaining vehemently about all the troubles in his life.

I think such emphasis is necessary in our translation of these words because of the intense and immense anguish in the psalm, which we observed in the previous chapter. We must be realistic about the terrible pain of those who have been hurt by the ones they have loved most. There is no easing of that pain in any simple way. The wounds inflicted by those closest to us seem to negate any possibility of healing. In this overwhelming anguish the psalmist cries out—and so do we.

The poet does not cry out just once in a while, either. He cries out morning, noon, and night. These words do not merely signify three particular times of prayer in one's day—when we arise, when we go to sleep, and before lunch. Rather, the poet is emphasizing symbolically that he cries out continually with the severe pain he is suffering.

The misconception that I want to combat is the well-intentioned advice of those who say, "Make your intercession or petition once, and then start thanking God for his answer." To be always thanking God for how he will work things out for our benefit is indeed a helpful habit. We can trust his promise that he is active to transform circumstances to bring good out of evil. However, I resist the phoniness of merely thanking God when we are still suffering overwhelming pain.

The danger of a theology that advocates only thanking rather than continuing our complaint is that such forced gratitude puts a coat of religiosity over our anguish and often inhibits the healing that mourning brings. When we are suffering from grief, we dare not suppress it—not even with religious piety.

I don't want to come down too hard on the "give thanks always" school of thinking because we are encouraged in other places in the Scriptures (Eph. 5:20 and 1 Thess. 5:18, for example) to give thanks continually in all things. I don't deny that principle at all; I believe that thanksgiving is a very effective tool for regaining a godly perspective on what is happening in our lives.

But the danger is that we won't adequately deal with the confusion and grief that afflict us if we don't also recognize in the Scriptures the presence of texts like this one. As long as we are struggling with the pains of our existence in a sin-sick and broken world, we should be real about those pains with God. Besides, lamenting to him is one of the best ways to sort out our observations and determine their truth.

In light of the confusion arising from the many varying philosophies about prayer, a student asked me how often to pray for a particular request. As long as our mind is not settled about an issue, we might as well be honest with God and pour out our feelings about it. Why compound our struggles by being phony with him?

I think this is especially important when we wrestle with loneliness. Though I have often prayed about it and have often also come to peace about it, I still become distraught sometimes. Tonight I experienced such a crash.

I had spent a two-day Thanksgiving vacation with the family of one of my friends from Seattle. Though a stranger in their midst, I had felt at home in the conversations. Thanksgiving dinner was especially delightful because of the large family gathering, the fragrant aromas, the many specialities of the season. Several of us had enjoyed a long, leisurely walk in the crisp fall air. I had even been able to help them in a time that was tough emotionally, so I felt useful and loved.

But I came home to an empty and very cold house. Everyone else was gone for the Thanksgiving vacation. As I struggled for more than an hour to light the fire in my wood stove, I kept clobbering myself with logs, burning my fingers trying to position the kindling, and inundating the office with smoke. I don't usually have any trouble with the stove, so frustration kept mounting until I finally screamed, "God, I wish I didn't have to be alone."

There wasn't unbearable pain in that aloneness, but the irritations accentuated the cold silence of this big house, and I mourned for the six-hundredth time that I didn't have anyone to share the rest of the holiday with me. I am greatly relieved that I can in the evening and in the morning and in any of the many noontimes cry out that distress to God.

That freedom to be real is especially comforting because, as the poet continues, Yahweh "hears my voice." When we complain continually to those around us, they get tired of listening and sometimes close their ears to our pleas. In contrast, Yahweh will always listen to our cries, even if they are ascending on the same subject for the skillionth time.

The NIV translates the verb for "hearing" as a continuing state of affairs. In keeping with the faithfulness of his character, the LORD will always listen. Furthermore, if we, in turn, listen for his voice when we cry, we will be able to sort out our grief, grow from it, and, in the meantime, hear his comfort and strength to endure.

Perhaps Peter was thinking of verse 22 from Psalm 55 when he penned his well-known line, "Cast all your anxiety upon him for he cares for you" (1 Pet. 5:7). When the psalmist urges his readers to "cast your cares on the LORD," he uses a Hebrew verb that means "to throw or fling" and a noun that means "that which is given to a person." All the things that compose our existence—including the terrible grief caused by the close friend who has turned against us—we are to fling upon Yahweh rather than taking them upon ourselves.

This is a tremendous invitation, yet we hesitate to accept it. Furthermore, when we do accept it, sometimes we do so only momentarily. Soon after flinging everything at his feet, we pick up those burdens again and carry them back with us into our thoughts and lives. Why are we so unable to take God at his word and thoroughly place our cares upon him?

Part of the reason, it seems, is that we haven't learned the assurance of the escape, "in the evening, in the morning, and at middays I cry out in distress." Every time we are afflicted by those same old thoughts, we are invited to cast them back *again* upon Yahweh. When we develop that habit and turn over into his hands whatever grieves us, upsetting thoughts will afflict us less.

It is a matter of disciplining our thoughts. Either we can turn inward and struggle with them in our own minds and spirits, or we can cry them out to the LORD and experience his sustaining.

That is the assurance of the poet, and it is reinforced once again by an emphatic pronoun. The Hebrew says, literally, "And he himself will sustain you." The verb *sustain* is an elaborated form that means "to nourish, to endure." In other words, when God sustains us, he does not merely prop us up. His nourishment enables us to endure. When we cast our burdens upon the LORD, they might not go away, but we will be able to stand them.

That word of comfort gives us an answer when we are betrayed by those we trust. Since there seems to be no ultimate healing for such a deep wound, we find hope from the fact that in the grief of that death we will be sustained.

That truth began for me a process of healing. When I finally learned that I didn't have to "get past" the pain of betrayal, then I could, in the midst of it, rely more thoroughly on Yahweh to sustain me in it.

The pain is there. We cannot chase it away; we cannot deny its existence; we cannot even cope with it successfully. But we can cry it out to Yahweh, and he will hear. When we fling the burden of that pain upon him, he will grant the relief that enables us to bear that pain constructively.

Yet the poet offers an additional word of assurance beyond that. I suggest a translation of the original Hebrew that makes the final phrase of verse 22 fit more thoroughly into the context as we have discovered it. Rather than, "he will never let the righteous fall," the text might be saying, "he will not give forever a shaking to the righteous." We can't say that the righteous will never fall; we have all experienced falling. But the point is that such falling will never last the whole lifetime.

The Hebrew text begins with the word *not.* Then comes the

phrase, *will he give*, followed by a phrase that means literally "to forever." In other words, "not for always will he give us over to the shaking," which is the negation of security and comes from a verb meaning "to totter or slip." When we are rattled by the experiences of our lives, the LORD will not let us be battered by them indefinitely.

God does not push us, but sometimes in his wisdom he does allow us to fall. However, he will not let us be trampled in the dust when we are down. The more we learn to cast our cares on him, the more we will experience his sustaining to keep us from falling or to hasten our recovery.

The key lies in the evening, morning, and noontime crying out to Yahweh. Peter's expression of casting our care on him continues, "for he cares for you" (1 Pet. 5:7). The Living Bible translates that phrase, "for He is watching over everything that concerns you." All the little details of our lives, even the most minor of falls, are noticed by his infinitely loving and caring eyes. He can't get us out of his mind. When we call upon him all the time—morning, noon, and night—then we can't get him out of ours, either.

FOR FURTHER MEDITATION

1. What is the importance of thanksgiving when I am suffering?
2. In what ways has Yahweh liberated me lately and given me plenty of space?
3. What is the value for me of crying out to Yahweh whenever I am feeling distress?
4. How do I know that he will hear?
5. What does it mean to cast my cares upon Yahweh? to cast them again?
6. How have I experienced his sustaining when I have done so? How have I failed to experience that sustaining because I have taken the cares back again?
7. Why is it important to acknowledge the reality that we will fall? Why is it encouraging that Yahweh will not let us suffer the shaking forever?

9. It's All Right to Be Afraid

When I am afraid
I will trust in you.
In God, whose word I praise,
in God I trust; I will not be afraid.
What can mortal man do to me?

Psalm 56:3–4

"To be heroic doesn't mean you aren't afraid." Initially that comment surprises us, but then its truth sets us free. The person who is not afraid in a dangerous situation usually doesn't really know what is going on. The person who is aware of all the circumstances and proceeds anyway is the truly courageous person.

To be Christians does not necessarily mean that we are not afraid. In our desire for discipleship we struggle to be more trusting and with regret that we aren't more so. We're ashamed that we haven't reached the spiritual maturity that we feel we ought to have attained. Then we feel lonely because we're not strong enough as Christians really to belong. Moreover, fear and loneliness are mutually strengthening: the more we feel lonely, the more we get afraid, and greater fear makes us feel more alone because others don't seem to share our fears.

Into the midst of this escalation of both fear and loneliness, the words of Psalm 56 bring great comfort to us—especially because they follow Psalm 55, which is so vivid about the pain of having our trust betrayed. Now, the great hero David admits honestly that at times even he is afraid. It is in those times that his trust in Yahweh is particularly developed.

In his introductory comments for *69 Ways to Start a Study Group and Keep It Growing,* Larry Richards stresses the need to talk with fellow Christians about both what he calls the dynamic and the static levels. If we speak only about the "dynamic" action of God in our lives—that is, the victories that his presence brings to us, then we run the danger of being phony

—because that is not all there is to anyone's existence. But, if we concentrate only on the "static" level, which is our human failings, then we get terribly discouraged and wonder if being a Christian has any effect on our daily lives.

In Bible study groups both dimensions of our existence must be balanced in our conversations together. That way we can identify with each other as human beings who have needs and failings and desires and motivations, but we can also see the effect of God's action in our lives. We can be encouraged both by what he is doing in others and by the progress we notice as we yield ourselves to his work in us. The poet achieves a good balance with, "When I am afraid," as a preface to the declaration, "I will trust in you."

More than our English translations, the Hebrew construction emphasizes that trust can characterize those times when we are afraid. The sentence begins with the construct *the-day-of*, which means, when put together with a verb in the imperfect or incompleted action tense, "in the day when." In other words, at the very time when we are afraid, that is the time for trust.

Usually in times when we feel fear, we try hard not to be afraid. Attempting to push it under, however, can bring a volcanic explosion of fear when we can no longer keep the lid on all that anxiety that we've been struggling to keep corked. The concept in this psalm, by contrast, is a managing of emotions: dealing with fear by accepting its reality and learning to trust in the midst of it.

In practical terms, this discipline of thought can free us from the panic of trying to control fear. A few weeks ago, I experienced dizziness more severe than my typical problems with low blood pressure. In the past, whenever I have tried to stop being afraid, that fear has exploded instead into worry about how soon I will be incapacitated by my handicaps. Needing to understand why I had almost collapsed on the kitchen floor of the home where I was staying, I couldn't merely dispense with heightened feelings of fear.

However, because I've been learning this concept of managing emotions and have been meditating on this verse, I tried to keep praying like this: "LORD, I am afraid of what is going on in my body right now. I don't know why it is malfunctioning like this, and I'm scared about it. But I do know that you are a God who takes care of me, and I know that you are here to help me with this. Teach me to trust you even though what I feel right now is fear."

Though this example might sound silly, that freedom to be afraid released me from the panic that usually compounds my problems; it enabled me to think more rationally about the situation. Though the symptoms weren't the usual ones, within a half hour I finally realized that this was a peculiar insulin reaction. Taking sugar eased the symptoms. Within an hour, I could function normally and lead the Bible study that was scheduled at the church I was visiting.

The whole process illustrated for me the validity of the psalmist's approach to fear. When we are scared, we are invited to concentrate on who Yahweh is and that he is trustable, rather than on the cause of our fears. We do not have to squelch the emotions that are an uncontrollable reality, but manage them so that they can be channeled constructively. Then we can actually delight in the presence of the LORD with us in the midst of whatever is so alarming.

We can react to fear in this way because we have complete assurance that Yahweh will take care of us. His covenant relationship with us has provided us with promises that are foundations for our trust. That is why the psalmist continues by saying, "in God, whose word I praise." His word is to be praised because it reveals to us the character of our faithful God. Scriptural accounts give us more than enough evidence that he is eminently worthy of our trust.

The term *word* means not only one's speech itself, but also the content of one's words. Thus, it can mean here, not only the record of God's promises in the Scriptures, but also the content of those promises, as well as Jesus who is the Word (see John 1:1–14) of both promise and fulfillment in the New Testament.

For the Old Testament people, the word was the instruction that they received concerning God's covenant relationship with them. Now, having the Scriptures recorded for us, we can continually turn to them to learn the content of God's promises to us so that we can rely on them in times of fear.

Furthermore, the discipline of memorizing the Scriptures can put the word in our thoughts, readily available for us to be reminded of the character of our God. Then we have something tangible to lean on—specific promises addressed to us to cling to when we are afraid.

After the emphasis on trusting God in our fears, the Hebrew text continues with an important progression that is not so noticeable in the English. In verse 3, which began with being afraid, the phrase "I will trust in you" uses an imperfect verb, which designates incomplete action: When we are afraid, we need to *keep* working on the trust. However, in the fourth verse, after the psalmist has emphasized that in God we have received the revelation of his word (for which we praise him), the verb *trust* is in the perfect tense, which designates completed action: Once we have learned that the God who is revealed to us in the word is trustable, then we can respond decisively with trust.

For this reason, the poet can continue, "I will not be afraid." Once our minds have moved through the progression of managing our fears by means of trust in Yahweh, we will come to the point where we are not afraid anymore.

In the final phrase of verse 4, there is this additional reason why we no longer have to be afraid: "What can mortal man do to me?" The Hebrew text uses a word that we often translate "flesh" to indicate frail or erring human beings as compared with God, who is omnipotent and omniscient. What can mere human assailants do to us when God is on our side?

We are impressed by the courage of Christian heroes who, though in danger of death, have gone boldly on with their ministries. Such saints serving in strife-ridden places have not been oblivious to the dangers inherent in their roles and geographical locations. Rather, they have worked through their fears and have come to the insights of this psalm. What can a mere human do to us, after all?

Jesus refers to this freedom from fear of human harm when he says, "I tell you, my friends, do not be afraid of those who kill the body and after that can do no more. But I will show you whom you should fear: Fear him who, after the killing of the body, has power to throw you into hell." Immediately thereafter he comforts us with this truth: "Are not five sparrows sold for two pennies? Yet not one of them is forgotten by God. Indeed, the very hairs of your head are all numbered. Don't be afraid; you are worth more than many sparrows" (Luke 12:4–7).

We frequently hear the contemporary expressions, "The only thing we have to fear is fear itself" or "You are your own worst enemy." We fail, however, to recognize the biblical roots of these expressions and thus don't recognize the larger truth of all that we have on our side. God said long ago that we do not need to be afraid of others. Disciplined study of this question, "What can mortal man do?" enables us to move more boldly and constructively into whatever produces fear in our own lives.

Are we afraid to tell others about our faith because of what they might think or how they might mock us for our stand? Are we afraid of economic struggles because of our Christian principles? Perhaps we might be fired if we refuse to cheat or if we won't automatically flunk a student who has problems that cause us concern. What can mortal man do to us?

Are we afraid of going to jail because of our protest for godly principles in the government? I just read a great letter from Jim Wallis, of the Sojourners community in Washington, D.C. Though in prison for protesting nuclear weapons, he wrote with a convincing boldness and Joy. What can mortal man do to us?

They might mock us or reject us, but what does that matter, anyway, when we are so profoundly undergirded by the promises of Yahweh? They might imprison us, but often that increases the power of our message about the love of God. We might be harassed in academic programs because we don't accept the vain philosophies of contemporary culture, but this can become a great vehicle for God's love to be shown and for us to learn what we really want to do with our lives.

Many people have been attracted to Christianity when human endeavors failed, drawn by the witness of those who know that mortals can't do anything to us that God doesn't allow and ultimately bring to our benefit. This is but one of the many words of assurance in the Scriptures we can turn to when we are afraid, so that we might learn to trust.

Psalm 56:3-4 shows us what to do with our fears. If we begin by looking at the character of the God in whom we trust and concentrate on trusting him even though we fear, then we will be able to move to thanksgiving for the truth of his word, which will set us free to trust without being afraid. Realizing that mere mortals cannot hurt us helps us in that discipline of mind: What can mortal man do when we have a God whose word can be trusted and whose promises are sure?

FOR FURTHER MEDITATION

1. When and why am I afraid?
2. What happens when I try to simply squelch that fear?
3. How can I learn to manage that fear instead?
4. How does the word of God give me hope as I trust in him?
5. How have I experienced the managing of fear successfully? How have I felt about my fear in the process?
6. Why do I not need to be afraid of what people can do? In what circumstances am I afraid, anyway? How can I get past those fears?
7. Why is the progression of verses 3 and 4 in Psalm 56 so important?

10. Our God Records Our Tears

Record my lament;
  list my tears on your scroll—
  are they not in your record?
Then my enemies will turn back
  when I call for help.
  By this I will know that God is for me.
In God, whose word I praise,
  in the LORD, whose word I praise—
in God I trust; I will not be afraid.
  What can man do to me?

Psalm 56:8–11

Thou has kept count of my tossings;
  put thou my tears in my bottle!
  are they not in thy book?
Then my enemies will be turned back
  in the day when I call.
This I know: that God is for me.

Psalm 56:8–9,
Revised Standard Version

Why is it that a child will cry wildly when her father is in the room, but if he ignores her and walks away, the crying ceases? The crying can be a plea for understanding. If it hasn't worked, the child will soon try some other means to get attention. But if someone who is concerned actively listens to the child, the crying ceases because it isn't necessary. The child feels understood.

The verses from Psalm 56 enable us to cease crying, not because it isn't working, but because we know that God is listening and cares and understands. God does indeed pay thorough attention to our tears and confusions.

The Hebrew text begins with a word that means "wanderings" and has the pronoun *my* attached. Since this is the only place that this noun occurs in the Old Testament, we see the poet's precision in choosing it to describe his situation. The word describes the aimless wanderings of a fugitive and pictures graphically the life of someone nobody knows.

The picture reminds me of a woman who lived with us here in our EPHESUS Community when it was still a home for crisis ministry. She came with hardly any money, stayed a few months, and suddenly left. After several months she came back, left her car with us, and went to Alaska. We couldn't reach her when she was there, but suddenly, long before the cannery season was over, she returned to get her car and was gone again. Her wanderings had no set destination, and we couldn't know her because our care couldn't follow her. Though some of her possessions are still here, we have no idea where she is and if or when she will ever come back. We care very much about her, but have no way to keep track of her.

This image is made poignant for me by my concern for her: "You, Yahweh, have taken account of my wanderings." Even though sometimes we might feel that no one really keeps track of us, though we might wander as far out of sight and mind as that houseguest, still Yahweh closely observes us. He really cares about every little thing that concerns us.

Differences in interpretations make the Hebrew text as muddled as the poet's confusion. The Revised Standard Version says that Yahweh "has kept count of my tossings." NIV translates the Hebrew concept as a "lament" to be recorded. The Jerusalem Bible uses the word *agitation*, whereas the New American Standard, alone, uses the idea of "wanderings." The point is that God cares about us. In the midst of our confusions, aimless wanderings, agitations, tossings, and lamentings, he is taking record.

The poet goes on to note how carefully He observes our pain. An imperative verb calls for the LORD himself to put our tears in his bottle. We know that he will do so, for the poet continues with the question, "Are they not in thy book?" (RSV) That last noun, rendered "book," is related to the verb *count* that is also used in this verse. Since it is a rare noun used in the Old Testament only here to mean "document or book of record," we know that the poet is implying that God has indeed kept accurate count.

The first verb, *count*, also forms a word play in Hebrew with the noun *wanderings*. These puns and root relations link the sentence together poetically to underscore the fact that God cares intimately for every little detail of our lives.

The command to God to "put thou my tears in thy bottle!" (RSV) is an arresting image. The child who cries in our presence wants us to share in her sadness. Similarly, our tears are usually easier to bear if only someone knows about them. If there could only be somebody significant to care that we have cried ourselves to sleep! The poet asks God to keep all those tears in his wineskin, lest they will have been cried in vain.

That picture can amuse even as it comforts. Imagine God's huge wine cellar, filled with rows and rows upon rows of wine skins. Each one is labeled with the name of an individual, and when that person cries He catches all the tears and stores them in the right flask. I sometimes think that he has had to use at least seventy flasks for me. Indeed, that is the point of the verse. No matter how extensive our confusions or wanderings or tears, God has cared intensely about them all.

When I was first alone after more than seven years of marriage, I was trapped in a deep depression that lasted for months. Caught up in my work of teaching the Scriptures at retreats on weekends, I found great Joy. But during the week at home alone, I often cried myself to sleep with wrenching sobs that lasted far into the night. It was especially comforting to me that God would really want to store up every tear in his bottle.

Because the Lord kept my tears in his wineskin, I knew that I would not drown in them. Though it seemed sometimes that I would be swallowed up by the billowing black clouds of despair, in the midst of them God gave always a sense of his presence to protect me. Ultimately, tears cannot overwhelm us because God has recorded them. That is why the poet can continue, "Then my enemies will be turned back in the day when I call." This "in the day" seems to parallel the phrase "in the day when I am afraid" that we considered in the previous chapter. When we call upon God, he will not let enemies triumph.

The stronger Hebrew phrase says, literally, "Then shall turn back [in fear or shame] the ones hating me in the day when I will cry out for help." Because God is on our side to record our tears and pain, they will be either terrified of the power he uses on our behalf or ashamed.

The concluding phrase of verse 9 proclaims even more assurance. "This I know: that God is for me" (RSV). We might not know any other comfort in the troubles of our lives, but this is not an empty promise: Our God is for us.

Tonight three people called me for counseling. As the last was concluding, she apologized for dumping so much bad news on me so late at night. I tried to assure her that, even though I had no specific answers for her struggles, I'm glad she talked through her griefs and sorted them out. Now I know more accurately how to pray for her, and I want to be as supportive as possible. We each, much more effectively, receive that care and support and listening ear from God.

The tragedy of our aloneness is that we have to bear its pain alone. That is not a redundant sentence; we must acknowledge that our sense of despair is multiplied by the fact that we bear it alone, which in turn increases the emptiness of the aloneness. Therefore, we intensely need assurance such as these words on a plaque given to me by Marguerite, who has faithfully stood beside me: "Don't forget: I'm your friend, no matter what."

The Covenant Yahweh is offering that comfort to us through the words of the poet David. Therefore, with confidence we can respond with the psalmist, "This I know: that God is for me."

As the Apostle Paul says, "If God is for us, who can be against us? He who did not spare his own Son, but gave him up for us all—how will he not also along with him graciously give us all things?" (Rom. 8:31b–32). If God is with us, will we lack anything else that is essential? (This question will be addressed more thoroughly in Chapter 15.)

Verses 10 and 11 return to the refrain lines that we studied in the previous chapter from Psalm 56:4, with one notable addition. Besides saying, "in God, whose word I praise" (a phrase from v. 4), this time the poet adds a parallel line, "in the LORD, whose word I praise." The doubling of the idea not only reinforces it, but also significantly adds the declaration that the one who is my God is Yahweh, the Covenant Keeper. Upon his promise we can rely.

The refrain reminds us that we can trust in God without fear, that mortal human beings cannot do anything to us that matters in light of our relationship with God. To read those phrases again after the assurance that God has recorded our tears and cares, our fears and prayers, is a double accentuation, since we now appreciate how much more is involved in his care for us.

We can trust Yahweh's word to us because he has listened and recorded our tears. His word contains the comforting hope that not only dries them, but also promises to take them away forever.

Therefore, we respond with thank offerings. The poet promises to fulfill his vows, and we turn with praise to use our lives in gratitude and Joy-full acclamation. After all, this is what we know: Our God is for us!

FOR FURTHER MEDITATION

1. When in my spiritual life have I felt like a wanderer?
2. How do I know that God knows and observes my wanderings?
3. How does it affect me to know that God cares about all the littlest details of my life? Does that scare me or make me glad? Why?
4. Why is it comforting to think that God would keep all my tears in his bottle?
5. What if my enemies aren't turned back right away in the day when I call?
6. How do I know that God is for me?
7. What progression do I see in this psalm between the first use of the refrain (v. 4) and the second (vv. 10–11)?

11. The Right Kind of Fear

Know that the LORD has set apart the godly for himself;
the LORD will hear when I call to him.
In your anger do not sin;
    when you are on your beds,
    search your hearts and be silent.   *Selah*
Offer right sacrifices
    and trust in the LORD.

                                        Psalm 4:3–5

Tremble and do not sin;
    Meditate in your heart upon your bed,
    and be still.   *Selah*
Offer the sacrifices of righteousness,
    and trust in the LORD.

                                        Psalm 4:4–5,
                        New American Standard Version

I had promised Tim that I would pray for him all the while that
he and the doctor discussed a new treatment for the failure of
his kidneys. For several years he has had to insert two huge
needles into his arm every Monday, Wednesday, and Friday, so
that his blood can be circulated through an artificial kidney for
more than eight hours per run. To change to a constant dialysis
across the peritoneum would free him from the lengthy routine
of setting up and coming off the run, the time-consuming care
of his dialysis machine, and the great chemical swings that leave
his body debilitated, but it held the risk of other complications.
I promised to pray as Tim weighed the advantages and disadvantages, but I didn't know how.

My usual meditation on the Psalms in the swimming pool
became an excellent vehicle for prayer. Though I had never
prayed for someone for two hours before, the experience grew
exciting when I thought about the phrase "Know that the LORD
has set apart the godly for himself." From Psalm 4 I learned
many important lessons about my relationship with my friend,
about how I can trust God to take care of him, and about the

proper place of fear in loneliness. First of all, the psalm assured me that Tim has been set apart by God. God has chosen him particularly and is using him for a special ministry. At that realization, a huge wave of confidence swept over me. I looked forward to all the lessons that Tim would learn in his decision and I would learn about prayer.

We are commanded to know this truth: "The LORD has set apart the godly for himself." The imperative implies that such knowledge will have important consequences in the way we live with it. One is in the next line: We can trust the LORD to hear when we call to him. Other consequences will be considered later in this chapter and in the next.

If Yahweh has set apart the godly for himself, we must ask if the godliness comes first and causes him to set apart those who exhibit it—or does his setting them apart create the godliness? In the context of the rest of the Scriptures, we can understand the text to mean that God is the actor in the setting apart. The text emphasizes this; it says specifically, with emphatic pronouns, "for himself." Godliness, then, is a gift first and then a response, not a characteristic that itself causes Yahweh's action.

To be set apart means to be made distinct, to be separated out. Sacred vessels were thus consecrated for use in the temple sacrifices. Different from other vessels because of their designation as sacred, they were used only for the purposes of worship.

The name *godly* comes from the Hebrew word *chesedh*, which we encountered in Chapter 1. God alone is characterized by perfect *chesedh*, the active, steadfast, faithful, loving-kindness of grace. Persons named *godly* are those who are pursuing such a character by diligently practicing God's loving-kindness. They are able to do so only because they have first passively received God's *chesedh* as it has been directed toward them. Thus, this first psalm phrase emphasizes the active passivity, that, paradoxically, characterizes the believer's life.

Tim illustrates this principle well. He has a very deep sense of the forgiveness of God. As a result, he actively seeks to incorporate that sort of love into his own life as he reaches out to minister to those around him. He would be the first to admit his failures, but he is always growing in godliness. God knows how far he has come since he has been His.

Some of us might be saying, "But I don't want to be separated. I'm already lonely; I don't want to be cut off any more." Fortunately, we are not separated to be alone, but to be part of a community, the people of God. Furthermore, we are separated, not only *from* the world (in the sense of cultural principles that we wouldn't choose because of our beliefs), but also *to* the LORD. He has called us apart for himself to make available to us all the gifts of his work in our lives. Our loneliness is eased by the care of the community into which he places us and by his caring gifts to us.

The first of those gifts, the assurance in this verse that he will hear us when we call to him, is much like the choosing of a beloved. One whose attention is fixed upon someone special will more eagerly listen to that person's requests than those of others.

It is our delight that God chooses each one of us that way. When a person chooses a beloved, everyone else is eliminated. But the special position and relationship with him that the LORD creates guarantees that he will hear each one of us when we call to him.

This assurance comforts us profoundly as we pray for each other. During the entire time I prayed for Tim, I rejoiced that the benefits of those prayers would be very apparent. Later, he said that he had felt thoroughly enfolded in God's wisdom as he deliberated with the doctor.

The next phrase is translated from the Hebrew in different ways in different English versions. The NIV urges, "In your anger do not sin." The Jerusalem Bible commands, "Tremble; give up sinning." The King James Version says, "Stand in awe, and sin not." The New American Standard Version renders the phrase, "Tremble, and do not sin." The first Hebrew verb says, literally, "come quivering," in the sense of fear, so the versions that use the idea of trembling convey the idea best.

Because the next command is to keep from sinning and the preceding concept is that of being set apart, I think we must understand quivering to mean awe or agitation, excitement, or perturbation. The verb for sinning is here the one that means "to miss a goal or way, to go wrong." Thus, the whole phrase introduces this very important, but often overlooked, issue in the Scriptures: the proper place for fear in the believer's life.

In his writings, Martin Luther ties the subject together closely with his understanding of the right use of the Law. The Reformer kept stressing that the Law cannot make us good, but it is a mirror to show us how bad we are and how much in need of a Savior. By its standard we can see that we utterly fail to act like the saints that we are by God's declaration. Though the LORD has set us apart as godly, our human nature keeps us from ever living like that.

That is why we must properly fear. When we realize with awe and trembling that we have no right to stand before a holy God (compare, for example, the experience of the prophet in Isaiah 6), then we will rejoice in the magnificent love that he demonstrated toward us in the death of Christ for us, his enemies (see Rom. 5:8).

The hymn "What Wondrous Love Is This" proclaims the mind-boggling fact "that Christ should lay aside his crown" in order to die for us. That seems almost too good to be true. With a proper sense of our unworthiness and inadequacy and failures, we sing in wonder at the immensity of God's love and respond to it with an eager desire not to sin.

We must always be warned against the wrong use of fear. God does not hold a threat over us all so that we are too terrified to misbehave or to omit a kindness. Rather, when we behold the wrath of God that we deserve and notice alongside it the immensity of love that rescues us from its punishment, in fear and awe we intensely desire to follow his desires.

To stress this balance, Martin Luther begins all of his explanations to the Ten Commandments with the phrase "We should fear and love God that we may not . . . " When we hold fear and love in a proper tension, our recognition of the wrath of God, which we fear because we deserve it, is overpowered by gratitude and wonder at the love that has borne that wrath for us. Thus, we can never take God's grace for granted, and thanksgiving, rather than stark terror, becomes the motivation for our good behavior.

The NIV loses the emphasis of the next clause when it begins with the idea of "when you are on your beds." The Hebrew phrase begins dramatically with the imperative, *search*. The godly person is instructed to consider within and to be silent. That command is also reinforced by the liturgical addition of the word *selah*, which most likely instructed the worshipers to pause for a while to consider what has just been said.

If the verse tells us what to do in our anger (as in the NIV), then in our hearts we are to search out the truth of what has made us angry, so that we respond without sin (see the context of Paul's quotation of this verse in Eph. 4:26). If the first word is *fear* or *tremble* (as in the NASV), then what must be considered in silence upon one's bed is a right relationship with God—the facts of one's sinfulness and the LORD's grace, and the response to that combination in a desire not to sin. Silence is the fitting response as we pause in wonder over those freeing realities. Just as the snowy splendor of magnificent mountains sometimes overwhelms us into silence, so the immensity of God's towering grace calls us to be still in awe before him.

Silence also expresses our shame and humility and acceptance. I almost wrote the word *resignation*, but I don't think such a negative passivity should characterize our silence. Rather, we wait hopefully, eager to learn more of who the LORD is, very much in the manner of this command from Psalm 46: "Be still and know that I am God" (46:10).

The interpretation "fear and do not sin" is reinforced further by the next phrase of the psalm. The poet continues, literally, "Offer the sacrifices of righteousness. And trust in Yahweh." In the last chapter, we learned about trusting as our reaction to being afraid. Here trust is the corollary to our offering sacrifices of righteousness.

We cannot be righteous by ourselves. Being righteous before God, just like godliness, is granted to us when the LORD sets us apart for himself. The Old Testament people who heard these words obediently offered the specific sacrifices of righteousness commanded by the Law, but those sacrifices were not sufficient to make them righteous. They were instead a reminder that one was coming who would be the perfect sacrifice and make righteousness available to us as a gift.

For us in the New Testament era, the requirements of specific sacrifices no longer apply, since Jesus has fulfilled them for us. But the exhortation to offer sacrifices of righteousness is for us an invitation to respond to Christ's sacrifice of himself with lives that seek what is right. Paul's exhortation to "offer your bodies as living sacrifices, holy and pleasing to God—which is your spiritual worship" (Rom. 12:1) is the New Testament modification of this verse from the Psalms.

The best part of our offering is to trust Yahweh. What he desires from us most of all is that we believe that his love is given to us freely, without our earning it in any way.

Because God has set us apart for himself, we want to respond by choosing righteous ways to fulfill God's will. For those of us who are lonely, this is a call to morality, an invitation to servanthood, an exhortation to give ourselves fully into whatever God might call us to do as we care for those around us.

In our trusting, we realize that our sacrifices are perfectly acceptable to him. That sets us free to respond even more thoroughly. Moreover, in offering ourselves first to God and then to others, we are often to our delight set free from loneliness to find new purpose and fulfillment and wholeness. (This will be considered further in later chapters, but is introduced here by the implications of our text.)

The final command to "trust in the LORD" actually completes our study of Psalm 56 and the progression that we have considered there from being afraid and still trusting to being not afraid (see Chapters 9 and 10). The absence of the wrong kind of fear is now matched with the understanding of the proper kind of fear, the kind that enables us to choose not to sin. We are set free from fears that would inhibit us and given right fears that keep us in check. We are thus liberated to offer ourselves as living sacrifices—holy and pleasing to God—because the LORD has set apart the godly for himself.

FOR FURTHER MEDITATION

1. What does it mean that Yahweh has set me apart for himself?
2. What does it mean that I am godly?

3. How does God's setting me apart give me assurance that he will hear me when I call?
4. How does the proper kind of fear keep me from sin?
5. What is the appropriate balance of fear and love?
6. What will be the result if I consider these things and am silent upon my bed?
7. What does the idea of "offering sacrifices of righteousness" mean to me?

12. Joy When Nothing Seems to Be Good

Many are asking, "Who can show us any good?"
Let the light of your face shine upon us, O LORD.
You have filled my heart with greater joy
 than when their grain and new wine abound.
I will lie down and sleep in peace,
 for you alone, O LORD,
 make me dwell in safety.

Psalm 4:6–8

Even the comic strips aren't funny these days. Several find black humor in the troubled economy or in the immorality of our times; some jab at such governmental actions as cutting support for people on welfare. Instead of bringing laughter, the "funnies" show us that the world isn't very funny. Underneath all of the sad humor seems to lurk the question, "Is there anything good anywhere?"

David's world in Psalm 4 is a similar culture of despair. When the godly are suffering distress, when the world is filled with delusions and idolatry (see vv. 1b and 2), the poet hears the people around him asking, "Who can show us any good?"

We see a search for good in the large shopping malls that glut the American landscape. Stores filled with trinkets and perfumes, the latest styles and gadgets, offer us "just the thing" to lift our spirits forever. Even some of the names of the stores suggest that we might be able to buy happiness there.

I listened to some Christmas advertisements on the radio before getting up this morning, and their pressures filled me with a terrible sadness. "See your little girl's eyes light up when she receives this doll for Christmas." "What fashions have you selected for the Christmas parties this year?" and "Let me tell you what to serve at the party everyone will be talking about till next Christmas." When all the right kinds of clothes and entertainments are failing to produce lasting happiness, many are asking, "Can anyone show us any good?"

The verb *asking* in verse 6 is a Hebrew participle, which indicates a state of being or continuous action. People keep on asking for good somewhere, somehow, because they are constantly becoming dissatisfied with what they find.

The psalmist offers a solution tied to the principle that Yahweh has set apart the godly for himself (as discussed in the last chapter). The first sentence that follows the agonizing question in this psalm says, literally, "Lift up upon us the light of your face, Yahweh." The Hebrew imperative asking God to lift up his countenance upon us comes from an attitude of humility. The poet, asking for this sign of God's kindness, is fully aware that only by God's loving action and lifting up is the gift of his light bestowed.

"The light of your face," probably an allusion to Numbers 6:26, is a graphic image to describe God's shining concern for his people. We experience that image vividly in human terms when someone who really cares about us looks at us. A few days before working on the revision of this chapter I returned from a four-day trip to California that had turned into three weeks of recuperating from emergency surgery. The shining radiance on the faces of my friends who met me at the airport showed me the fullness of their love for me.

The poet's request for Yahweh to lift up the light of his face upon us uses human terms we can understand to describe a divine radiance that is inexpressible. When the LORD's face shines upon us, we know that we will receive all the fullness of his gifts. Inevitably will come a genuine Joy that is available only to God's people.

This Joy that Yahweh gave "in my heart," the poet declares, is greater than all the happiness others experience when their grain and new wine abound, because it is based on facts, not merely emotions. *Heart* in the Hebrew designates what is grasped by the will. The universal search for happiness has no satisfaction apart from a genuine personal relationship with the LORD; furthermore, such a relationship produces a Joy deeper than can otherwise be experienced.

I have been capitalizing the word *Joy* when writing about that concept ever since I first wrestled through to an understanding of the biblical idea more than ten years ago. At that time I was leading a Bible study on Paul's letter to the Philippians at the University of Idaho, where I worked in campus ministry. One of the participants in that group couldn't understand how the passage, "Rejoice in the Lord alway, and again I say, Rejoice" (Phil. 4:4), could be possible. The following "three-level theory" illustrates Paul's frequent exhortations to Joy.

The normal person's life has two levels of reality: the experiences of happiness, and those of sorrow. Our two hands can illustrate these two aspects of life. The top hand is the happiness level of life, which occurs when all goes well—when a person has plenty of money, a loving companion, good relations with parents or boss, straight A's in school, a smoothly running household, and so forth. The other hand, the lower level, is the sorrow side of life, when things aren't going so well—when a person is fighting with his or her spouse, getting lousy grades, drowning in a shambles of a household, not getting along well with others, or running out of money. Everyone has experienced both of these levels of existence at various times and to a greater or lesser degree.

The Christian, however, has a third level of existence. At this point, place both hands on the floor of the room—the happiness one on top of the other. Imagine that the floor is infinite, stretching on beyond the ends of the room forever. Imagine the floor as powerfully hard, like rock that cannot be broken through. This floor is the basis for the Christian's other two hands of existence. It stands for one simple, basic fact: the reality that Jesus Christ rose from the dead and thereby made possible for all time our acceptance by God. Nothing can crack that fact; nothing can destroy the eternal victory over death that it entails. The Scriptures call this Joy: a confident reliance upon the infinite, uncrackable resurrection fact.

The Easter fact brings Joy for at least three major reasons. First of all, Christ's Resurrection is proof that his fulfillment of life and death was sufficient to substitute for our imperfect life and our just death; therefore, we know that our sins are forgiven and that we have been made acceptable to God. Second, because Christ rose from the dead, we know that we, too, shall rise and live eternally with him. Finally, the victory of the Resurrection assures us that we, too, can find strength for our everyday struggles.

Lift your two hands into the air, and you see the existence of the unbeliever. Tossed about by circumstances, the two levels float around with nothing substantial as their base. Take away the happiness hand (when earthly pleasures fail and problems multiply), and all that remains is the hand of sorrow, being battered by the storms and tempests of change and disappointments.

Next, turn to look at the Christian, whose levels of happiness and sadness are permeated with the Joy of that infinite, never-to-be-cracked resurrection floor. Pretend that everything has gone wrong in the believer's life. Take away the top level of happiness so that all that remains of the original two levels is the hand of sorrow. Yet look! Underneath is that level of Joy that no one can take away.

How large is that hand of sorrow compared to our infinite floor? The Apostle Paul writes, "I reckon that the sufferings of this present time are not worthy to be compared to the glory which shall be revealed in us" (Rom. 8:18).

The fact of the Resurrection, proving the reality of God's love for us, remains unshaken. I felt enfolded in that love while recovering from that emergency surgery in a strange city far from home, and it created a Joy so great that the greatest amounts of sorrow just didn't seem large any longer.

To go further with our illustration, we need only spread the fingers of the hand of sorrow to see the greatness of the Joy underneath. The Apostle Paul proclaims, "In all things God works for the good of those who love him, who have been called according to his purpose" (Rom. 8:28). Even the fingers of sorrow in our lives draw Joy from the spaces between them as God weaves their elements together into a harmonious whole working together for good.

Joy is not merely an abstract concept; the poet praises God for filling his heart/will with a genuine reality. Even so, Joy undergirded my life even in the saddest days when I was first alone. For months I was sustained by the hope that someday all my sorrow will be swallowed up in the Joy of my own resurrection into an eternal life free from pain and heartbreak. The hand of sorrow is so small compared to that infinite floor. And meanwhile I have seen over the past four years how God has taken my sorrow and turned it into benefits in my present life and ministry. Underneath the hand of sorrow is a Joy that permeates grief and changes it into good, not only for myself, but also for others.

We do not have to slap the top hand of superficial happiness onto our existence and pretend that all is well when it is not. Happiness is temporal, dependent upon the circumstances that create it. Joy is eternal, dependent upon the accomplished fact that Christ has risen from the dead and made our relationship with God an established reality.

Human "corn and wine"—or any other devices for that matter—might make us happy for a while, but that soon passes away. (See Chapter 6 of my first book, *To Walk and Not Faint.*) In bright contrast, the true Joy created by our relationship with the LORD can never pass away.

I don't think that to be a Christian necessarily means that we will be happy. For those of us struggling with loneliness, there are many times when we cannot be happy. But we *can* "rejoice in the LORD alway," because he does indeed lift up the light of his face upon us.

We can also know his peace, the poet declares. In verse 8 he says he will lie down and sleep in *shalom*. In Chapter 26 we will consider *shalom* more thoroughly, but here we note that biblical peace goes hand in hand with Joy. As our relationship with God keeps enabling us to deal with the sorrows of our lives, we will have enough tranquility, the poet anticipates, both to lie down and to sleep. We will not be kept awake by the agitations of the world (v. 4). In our silence we will have come to trust the LORD (see the previous chapter).

Yahweh alone can enable us to dwell in "safety." The Hebrew noun for safety is related to the verb *trust* that we have encountered in many of the Psalms. There is no security in the things of the world, just as there is not happiness. Therefore, by means of a noun that signifies "isolation" or "separation," this final verse emphasizes that no one else but Yahweh alone is able to create for us that kind of safety. Not only can we be awake with him in Joy unspeakable, but we can also sleep in him with peace illimitable.

FOR FURTHER MEDITATION

1. How do I see the quest for happiness manifested in the society around me?
2. How can I be bold enough to ask God to lift up the light of his face upon me?
3. What does the image of the light of his face convey to me?
4. What is the Joy of the LORD? What is the difference between happiness and Joy?
5. How is it possible to rejoice always, as Paul exhorts?
6. How does my relationship with Yahweh enable me to lie down and sleep in peace?
7. Why is it that only Yahweh can make me dwell in safety?

13. The Right Kind of Boasting

I will extol the LORD at all times;
  his praise will always be on my lips.
My soul will boast in the LORD;
  let the afflicted hear and rejoice.
Glorify the LORD with me;
  let us exalt his name together.
                              Psalm 34:1–3

I don't feel like writing this chapter. Though I can talk about these texts with others and communicate their ideas, the disciplines of study and organizing and writing all have to be done alone. Tonight the solitude of my work is making me feel particularly lonely.

Hoping to find some motivation to get to work, I called Tim for help, but he is feeling ill earlier than usual on his dialysis run and doesn't feel like talking. So I sit here and cry and watch the pity party develop. My fingers are sore. My feet are cold. My head is swimming. I would give anything to have someone to comfort me, to care and say, "I love you."

Just now I called up my prayer partner, Elaine, and told her I was in trouble emotionally. We talked together about extolling the LORD at all times. Discussing the themes of this chapter with her, I experienced the great benefit of the disciplines of prayer and fellowship that Psalm 34 espouses. The two support each other.

According to the title of Psalm 34, David wrote it when he had to feign insanity to escape from Abimelech. (The account is given in 1 Samuel 21:10–22:2. Differing records cause some confusion over his enemy's name. Probably the title of this psalm uses the dynastic family name of the king, whose personal name was Achish, king of Gath.) After David fled from Saul, he began to gather around him others who were oppressed. Most likely this psalm was written much later, after he had had time to reflect on the experience, his reaction to it, and its value for his life. The poem is obviously a studied one because it is an acrostic, which means that each verse begins with the next letter of the Hebrew alphabet.

As David looks back, he recognizes that Yahweh was in ulti-mate control of his life, and, therefore, he responds to God's love with these words of praise. His words urge us to choose the discipline of remembering the character of the God who cares about us. Even when we don't feel like praising, there is com-fort in the very habit.

David begins with a verb that has its root in the word mean-ing "to kneel or to adore with bended knee." In the intensive (Piel) form, this verb means "to bless, to extol." Its rooting suggests that extolling the LORD at all times is based on humil-ity, our own kneeling recognition that in spite of evidences to the contrary Yahweh is always worthy of our praise. We have considered in previous chapters this act of conscious intention-ality. Though the normal nastinesses of everyday life will tempt us away from extolling the LORD "at all times," the choice to praise is made easier, not only by Yahweh's supreme worthi-ness, but also by our surprise at the benefits, which we will discuss later in this chapter.

"Continually his praise in my mouth" is the literal parallel line of the opening sentence of the poem. The noun for "conti-nuity" is used here as an adverb, and there is no verb to accen-tuate this state of being: that adoration and thanksgiving will surely be in our mouths.

Because I get discouraged about the peridontal problems that have caused my jaws to deteriorate, I kid my Christian dentist that I have named my partial bridges His Praise, since they are continually in my mouth. That joke has turned out to be a good reminder when, after hours of teaching, they cause some irritation. At those times, their very presence, even though painful, nudges me to keep my words constant in re-flecting worship.

In the second verse the psalmist declares that his soul will boast in Yahweh. The Hebrew emphasizes "in Yahweh" by placing it first. The statement reminds me of Paul's comments about glorying only in the cross of Christ: Nothing else is worth our boasting (see Phil. 3:7–11 and Rom. 5:1–11).

The statement that "my soul" shall boast in the LORD is

much larger than we might think at first. As we saw in Chapter 4, the Hebrew word *nephesh* or "soul" means the whole being, the true essence of a person. In other words, with his deepest self the poet David recognizes that his boasting should be about Yahweh's character rather than his own.

The concept of boasting is easily distorted by Christians. We are so afraid of prideful boasting that we don't know how to do it right. To boast properly is to recognize humbly where credit is due. Thus, to boast in Yahweh means to point out to others what he has done and how we have seen him at work in our lives.

Too often the "testimony" given in worship elevates, improperly, the person doing the speaking. We are not left feeling, "What a wonderful God that person has." Good testimony leaves everyone knowing *God* better.

The purpose of our boasting is made clear by David's next line, which says, literally, "The afflicted ones will hear and be joyful." We need more genuine testimony in the Church, so that those who are weak or humbled or oppressed can be glad with us. The two Hebrew verbs, *shamah* and *samach*, make a pun in this phrase to reinforce dramatically their message. Hearing (*shamah*) is closely related in both sound and experience to being joyful (*samach*).

David's words urgently call us to apply them actively in our Christian circles. If we only appreciated the immense value for others that comes from speaking about what the Lord is doing in our lives, we would do it more often and, thus, be further strengthened. What is the topic of conversation in the narthex of your congregation? Is there space in our worship services for rejoicing together in what God is doing?

The prevalence of support groups in our society indicates the need for finding strength in the positive experiences of others who have gone through what we are encountering. The Church could be a safe haven where the afflicted could be nurtured in hope.

The poetic parallels (two lines that offer corresponding perspectives on the same subject with synonymous words and phrases) underscore the importance of the fellowship of those who boast in the Lord (v. 3). The poet calls his listeners first to magnify the LORD with him. The verb means "to cause to become great." We can't make Yahweh great, but we can delight in making his greatness obvious to those around us.

We find it easy to praise our friends who are gifted. I like to show my housemate Julie's art to others or invite them to listen to her magnificent singing. Those who see or hear will undoubtedly benefit from her gifts.

In the same way, we gladly magnify Yahweh because we know that those who are introduced to his presence will greatly benefit. We have no doubts that God will faithfully prove himself worthy of praise to anyone who accepts the challenge to get to know him. Evangelism becomes a delightful privilege and a natural reaction. We don't raise Yahweh up; we simply enable others to see his prior elevation.

The poetic parallel, "Let us exalt his name together," makes the invitation more personal. Since the term *name* designates a person's character, to exalt Yahweh's name means to recognize his *chesedh* (steadfast loving-kindness) and all the other attributes we have been discovering in these chapters. The invitation is for us to do that together as a community in action. Since we each have our own unique perspective on God's character, we need each other to see more of what God is like.

The best part is that such glorying together in a bond of praise eases our loneliness. When I called my prayer partner earlier tonight, our "boasting" together about the faithfulness of God motivated me to begin writing. Soon the subject itself became so exciting to me that my fingers began to fly on the keys.

When I called Elaine back to tell her the good news that our togetherness had been exactly what I needed, we could again "glorify the LORD" together. Such a profound experience of the truth of this passage from Psalm 34 filled me with rejoicing—that Joy in the LORD that is our strength (Neh. 8:10b) and that is always the undergirding of our lives (see Phil. 4:4 and Chapter 12 of this book).

I just paused for a moment to check my wood stove and saw there a reinforcing image. Since I added another log a short while ago, the fire is burning much better now. One log can't burn very well alone, but when two are propped against each other, the fire adds a lot of warmth to my cold basement office. The togetherness of God's people causes our praise to burn more brightly.

If you were here with me, I'd pick you up from your chair and dance around the room with you to the accompaniment of the exuberant piano concerto that is playing on the radio right now. Exhilarating moments like this deepen my desire to keep the praise of God always in my mouth.

In the rough moments, when we can't crank ourselves up to get going, we don't have to manufacture our own Joy or pretend our energy. Renewal is readily available to us in the habit of praise. As we bless Yahweh, we are blessed. As we boast in his love, the recounting fills us with his presence. And when we do that together, we are doubly encouraged.

FOR FURTHER MEDITATION

1. Can we really praise Yahweh at all times?
2. When we lose the praise from our mouths how can we recover it?
3. What is the difference between proper and improper boasting?
4. Do the afflicted really hear and respond with rejoicing when I boast? What might be weak about my testimony? In what ways is it effective?
5. What friends do I especially like to invite to magnify the LORD with me?
6. If I don't have many such friends, how might I acquire some so that I could be strengthened by them?
7. How can my church help people to exalt the LORD's name together?

14. Radiance and Angels

Those who look to him are radiant;
  their faces are never covered with shame.
This poor man called, and the LORD heard him;
  he saved him out of all his troubles.
The angel of the LORD encamps around those who fear him,
  and he delivers them.

Psalm 34:5–7

I knew that my face was beaming. That embarrassed me a bit, but I couldn't help being pleased at the performance of the pianist. I had followed the music as my young friend had prepared for this concert. Consequently, I knew the tricky spots as they were successfully performed, and I felt a radiant delight in the pianist's mastery of the keyboard.

David uses a similar picture to describe the people of God. The original text says, literally, "They looked unto him and beamed." The first verb form stresses that they paid close attention. Looking to Yahweh with intensity caused them to beam. A figure for Joy, this second verb means "to shine or be radiant" and implies a natural response to what is observed. When the people of God look to him, they are made radiant by the wonder of his embracing love.

Immediately we think of Moses, who had to wear a veil over his face after he came down from being with the LORD on Mount Sinai for forty days and forty nights. The people could not look upon him because he was so radiant, according to Exodus 34:29–35 and 2 Corinthians 3:7–13. In the latter passage, Moses' secret is let out of the bag. After he had been down awhile, his face began to lose its radiance because he was no longer in the presence of God Himself.

Moses' need to wear the veil to hide his fading radiance reminds us to be continually in the presence of Yahweh. The radiance of which David speaks is not a once-given gift that lasts for all time, but a reflection of what we are observing. The more we look to Yahweh, the more we will continue to be changed into his likeness, from one degree of glory to another, as Paul stresses in 2 Corinthians 3:18.

At times I have not been radiant about my friend's piano performances. A high school student, he lacks self-discipline in practicing and sometimes plays poorly. Then my trust is put to shame (although I don't love him any less for that). In relationship with the LORD, however, we can trust our faces will never be put to shame. He will always be true to his character.

Pause with me to consider if we have ever been ashamed as we have looked to Yahweh. If, in our pain, we answer yes, we must look more deeply. Usually, we feel shamed because of our failure to keep looking, or we feel embarrassed because things don't turn out as we wish. Then we feel that God has let us down.

A young Christian woman may insist that, since God has promised to give her the desires of her heart, he must answer her prayer for a certain man to marry her. Her shame at the failure of her prayer is entirely of her own making, for surely she has not been regarding seriously the whole context of the LORD's promise. Her misunderstanding points out once again the need for consistent study of the Scriptures in their entirety.

Careful reading is also necessary for the next verse of the psalm, lest we misinterpret and feel again that God has failed us. The poet says, literally, "This poor one called, and Yahweh heard and from all his distresses he delivered him." The word for "poor one" is the same noun that we encountered in the previous chapter and means whoever is oppressed. David is most likely describing his own experience and uses the demonstrative *this* to point to his own crying out for the help of the LORD when his life was threatened by Abimelech.

The faithfulness of Yahweh (as we have seen it so often already in our study of the Psalms) is underscored by the fact that here again he has heard and delivered the afflicted one from all distresses. The final verb is the one that we studied in Chapter 8, which means "to give width or breadth to, to liberate." The word for "distresses" is the noun that we found (in Chapter 6) to mean "adversities" that come from being bound up or straitened. Yahweh has set this poor one free from those things that have created for him a narrowness.

We must read that carefully lest we complain that God hasn't set us free from all our struggles. The verb says that in those struggles Yahweh creates for us breadth and width so that we have enough space to stand firm. The particular adversities in which we find ourselves might not be taken away, but he gives us a way to escape so that we can endure (as Paul says in 1 Cor. 10:13).

These sentences are especially liberating for those of us who are single and lonely. If we said, "God has failed me. He has not given me someone to take away the agony of my loneliness," we would not be accurately understanding God's provision for us. He saves us out of all our troubles by giving us strength to hold on and friends to stand with us and by creating enough space so that we can handle our problems.

I will probably struggle with the problem of being alone for the rest of my life. Yet God never fails to give me means of encouragement, such as my prayer partner, Elaine, described earlier, who helped motivate me to write.

Sometimes it is music that invites us into God's presence. A call or a card from a friend may be what uplifts us. Sometimes merely the memory of something that a friend has said is sufficient. In our roughest moments we might have to reach out and ask someone for the comfort we need, but God does not fail to provide. I pray as we work through this book together that the faithfulness of God for your loneliness is becoming more and more real. Sometimes the LORD provides ways we would least expect, but, if our eyes and hearts are open, he has all sorts of surprises up his sleeve (as if he had a sleeve!).

My favorite surprise is the angels. Yesterday was the first Sunday of Advent, the beginning of the new liturgical year. Since this is the season of repentance in preparation for Christmas, I celebrate it by putting up an Advent calendar and wreath, a manger scene, and an angel choir.

We don't really understand angels and can't picture them. That is why I especially enjoy the wide variety of paper, yarn, ceramic, and straw angels who join my Advent celebration each year. The promise of Yahweh in Psalm 34 is that his encamping angel is around about the ones fearing him, to be an agent for the LORD's deliverance. My friends tease me that either God has given me extra angels or the ones assigned to me do double duty. With my physical handicaps and extensive traveling, divine protection by angels is not just a childhood fantasy for me.

The Hebrew phrase begins with the verb participle, *encamping*. This word stresses that in all his or her excellence, wisdom, and powerfulness, the messenger of Yahweh is continually with the ones fearing (in the sense of honoring) Yahweh. Then the prepositions for "around about" lead into the fact of deliverance. The angels' encamping around us makes it possible for them to draw us out of difficulties.

Sometimes the word *angel* in the Scriptures seems to signify a human being who functions as the messenger of God. We each know "encamping" persons who have been ministering angels to protect us and speak God's words to us. My secretary, Sandy, sometimes even cleans my bathroom or does the dishes for me to keep my hands free from cracking, so that I can type and lead music with my guitar, and to give me time for my study and writing.

The Scriptures also speak specifically of literal angelic beings, invisible warriors who guard us and fight for us. They are constantly at war with the "spiritual forces of evil in the heavenly realms" (Eph. 6:12). We have scattered glimpses of them in such diverse places as the call scene of Isaiah 6, the appearances to Zechariah and Mary in Luke 1, or the work of the angels in chapters 14 and 16, especially, of Revelation, but we never discover much about them.

One favorite story summarizes all we need to know about angels, anyway. When Elisha is in danger for his life, his awed servant panics because he can see only the horses and chariots of the Aramaean army surrounding the city of Dothan (2 Kings 6:8-23). When he cries to Elisha, the prophet calmly answers, "Those who are with us are more than those who are with them" (v. 16) and then prays for Yahweh to open the servant's eyes. Immediately he is amazed to see "the hills full of horses and chariots of fire all around Elisha" (v. 17). The protection of Yahweh was very real, even though not particularly described. Because the name *seraphim* (in the call scene of Isaiah 6) comes from the root meaning "fire" and, therefore, seems to mean "fiery beings," they might have been part of that hillside host.

Our problem is that we don't usually see them, either. We need the LORD to open our eyes to see his messengers for combating the pain of loneliness. They encamp around us to bring us the message of Yahweh's presence. When we are afraid because we are alone, we need to take angels seriously as the forces that God constantly provides to protect us and take care of us.

I think specifically again of my friend Sandy. When I came home from a speaking engagement in Minneapolis a few weeks ago with a severely painful ear infection, she met me at the emergency room, helped me get medicine and handle details, took me to her home, made supper for me, took care of me all evening, put drops in my ears, and then took me back to my own home, where I was alone for the week, and tucked me into bed. The next morning I awoke to her ministering care.

Thinking about her as I write this chapter has brought me tears of gratitude for all the angels that God has placed around me. Perhaps the study questions below can help you think further about the angels in your own life.

FOR FURTHER MEDITATION

1. What experiences have I had of being supernaturally cared for?
2. Who are the ministering angels in my life?
3. How have I seen that looking to Yahweh produces radiance?
4. Have I ever been ashamed of him in my relationship with him?
5. How have I seen that Yahweh has delivered me *from* my distresses, though not necessarily *out of* them?
6. How can I handle concepts, such as this one of angels, that seem terribly outdated and yet are specifically recorded in the Scriptures?
7. How have I had opportunities to be God's angel for others?

15. Tasting the LORD's Goodness

> Taste and see that the LORD is good;
>   blessed is the man who takes refuge in him.
> Fear the LORD, you his saints,
>   for those who fear him lack nothing.
> The lions may grow weak and hungry,
>   but those who seek the LORD lack no good thing.
>
> *Psalm 34:8–10*

In *How to Help a Friend*, Paul Welter offers an exercise for discovering one's primary learning channel. The test has sixteen items under each of three categories to determine whether a person learns best visually or through hearing or by touch/ movement.

For all the time I spend reading and studying, I would seem to be a visual learner. However, I was surprised that under that category and in the auditory column I checked only three items as applicable, whereas nine statements under the touch/movement category described my lifestyle. Evidently, I learn best in tangible ways. That discovery freed me from worrying about what had seemed an inordinate need to be hugged.

Finding our best learning channels can help us deal more effectively with our lonelinesses. Depending upon the kind of person we are, we will be comforted most by listening to a record, reading a book, or being with somebody who touches us with the love of God.

Perhaps David included this eighth verse in Psalm 34 just for touch/movement learners. He doesn't merely say, "Check out the goodness of Yahweh." He encourages us to "taste and see that the LORD is good." The verb *to taste* urges us to examine by experience, by jumping right into God's goodness. How can we know Yahweh is good unless we give him a try?

That statement is a strong motivation for evangelism. Many people have not come into a relationship with the LORD because they have never tasted of his goodness. They might have heard or read all kinds of things, but they have never had the opportunity to check it out in tangible ways.

Several years ago a Christian journal carried the story of a young woman who had become a believer because someone had challenged her to test whether the Scriptures worked. In practicing a principle that she had read about not retaliating against enemies, she discovered the truth of the Christian life.

When we are lonely, we wallow too easily in our pity parties. Knowing for sure that we will not be disappointed, David urges us instead to go tasting. Having experienced God's goodness fully, he can be confident that it will never fail.

The Lord's Supper provides Christians with an opportunity to taste God's goodness in three tenses—past, present, and future. While sharing the bread and wine, believers look back to what Christ actually did for us in the breaking of his body and the pouring out of his blood in death. In that tangible tasting we also experience Christ's presence in the present community of those gathered around the table. Finally, we look forward in that eating to the fulfillment of Jesus' promises that we will feast with him at the great banquets of heaven.

One of my best ways to ease loneliness is to invite others to share God's presence with me in a meal. Conversation, the delight of being together, and holding hands in prayer enable us to taste and feel the goodness of Yahweh.

In the poetic parallel of the eighth verse, David adds that the person who goes to Yahweh for refuge, in the sense of protection or shelter, will be blessed. In fact, the literal Hebrew phrase is more of an exclamation. The word *blessedness* is in a construct form to say, "Oh, the blessedness of the warrior who seeks refuge in him." This is a statement of tangibility also, for shelter and protection imply warmth and physical harboring.

Next, David urges us to fear Yahweh. The verb that occurred in Chapter 11 in our discussion of the biblical balance of love and fear (in the sense of terror at the wrath of God) is not the verb for fear that David uses in this psalm. In verse 7 and twice in verse 9, he chooses instead the verb that means "to reverence or to honor" him. Because of the context—the previous words about the blessedness of those who take refuge and the next statement that those who fear lack no good thing—we can hear in this word *fear* an invitation to thankfulness and praise. When we honor God, we learn to recognize his goodness in all that is around us, and in that reverent awareness we are more likely to respond with gratitude.

The ones who are to fear him are his saints. That name reminds us that God has chosen us to be set apart as his people. In doing so, he has given us that very quality of set-apartness that is his. The scriptural pictures of God's holiness, such as the scene in Isaiah 6, are awesome visions. The prophet was filled with fear and horror and shame at his own sinfulness when he observed the holiness of God in his majestic enthronement and heard about it in the calling of the angels. You might want to read that chapter at this point and then meditate upon it to try to imagine the magnificence of God's holiness. Whenever we confront the perfection of God, we, too, are forced to fall on our knees and cry out, "Woe is me! I am annihilated." Like the prophet, we also are persons of unclean lips, and we dwell among people who are the same.

Yet the Joy of our faith is that God has made us holy because Jesus has lived perfectly in our place. That is why Paul addresses his letters to the "saints" of the various New Testament churches.

I have often asked participants at retreats to raise their hands if they are saints, but I have yet to find a group in which everyone does. For some reason we Christians have not yet learned that our sainthood is something that we already possess by God's declaration. Its reality does not depend upon whether or not we act like the saints that we are.

The Joy of our relationship with God, furthermore, is that he continues to enable us to act more like the saints we are by his perfect love and forgiveness and affirmation. Nevertheless, the fact of our sainthood remains, whether or not we are living it out.

Therefore, we who are rejoicing in that sainthood want, of course, to fear the LORD. We want to give him the proper honor and to receive the holiness he is creating in our lives.

David continues by recording the promise that those who are saints honoring Yahweh will lack nothing. That we will have no need of anything is hard to believe when we are lonely. We say,

"But I lack a friend" or "I long for someone to care for me intimately." Is David telling us a lie?

Why does God sometimes seem to deny us what we need most deeply? Is David just speaking about food-and-shelter kinds of things? We might think that because of the way he continues with the subject of lions.

I don't think the poet is speaking only of suffering from lack of food. Rather, it seems to me that David chose lions for his illustration because they symbolize bloodthirstiness and power. Even in their forcefulness, David says, they might be in want and go hungry. In other words, power is not the means by which our needs are going to be met. We will not find a person to satisfy our longing by any manipulation, exploitation, vindication, or bloodthirstiness.

Rather, David continues, the ones seeking Yahweh will not lack any good thing. The verb *seeking* in this tenth verse is the same one that David used in verse 5. There, the word means to seek deity through prayer and worship, to come into the presence of Yahweh in order to know him.

David's assertion is very carefully constructed to remind us that only by honoring Yahweh do we not lack any good thing. We might lack things that we think are good, but if we are seeking Yahweh's purposes, we will not miss anything that *is* good for us.

A fantasy, *The Tower of Geburah,* illustrates this point well. A child, Wesley, adventuring in another world, encounters Gaal, the Shepherd, who corresponds to Jesus. In a time of great danger they converse intensely about whether fighting evil is worth the effort when the venture might not be successful:

[Wesley:] "I suppose you want me to say that it's always worthwhile to fight evil even if you know you're going to lose. But that doesn't make sense. Yet you want me to say it does."

[Gaal:] "You seem to know a lot about what I am thinking. What I really wonder is whether you trust me or not."

"Trust you?"

"Yes, you seem to suspect that I do wrong to send you on a dangerous mission like this."

"It sounds awful when you put it that way."

"And I think for the moment that you're going to have to trust me even though I don't tell you all that's going to happen."

"But Gaal, of course we trust you."

"You mean you believe I know what I'm doing?"

It would have been insulting to say no, so Wesley uncomfortably said, "Yes, I suppose so—I mean—*yes.*"

"Do you think I don't care about you? Am I, perhaps, not a shepherd after all?"

As Wesley looked into Gaal's eyes he knew deep down inside himself that Gaal *did* care. What's more, he suddenly knew that Gaal knew what he was doing. He also knew that his questions had been pretty insulting to Gaal. He felt small and cheap.

"Then do as I bid you. The dangers are real, so beware of all I told you. It is not for you to see into the future, only to live in the present moment. And that involves being able to trust me." *

If the LORD were here and we looked into his eyes, we, too, would see that he cares for us after all. Even though he seems to have neglected something that would be good for us, he does know ultimately what is best.

Once again, we are thrown back upon the character of God. Is he good or isn't he? Sometimes we don't see that goodness, but we are invited to try it out—to search for it, in fact—because it is there. We can be sure that if anything were best for us, we would not lack it. Therefore, if we do not have a person to comfort us or to hold us, then for some reason that is not best.

That sounds like a cruel thing to say. But I'm learning that it is true. For all the times I long for someone to help me, I realize in my wiser moments that God really wants me to learn to trust him, to turn to him for eternal comfort that will not pass away. If we continue to seek him and to be open to what he wants to teach us, we will learn why certain things are withheld.

Nevertheless, some things we will never understand. That is why Gaal's words are so piercing. Sometimes it is necessary to simply rest in what is happening today and not worry about the future—or about understanding the reasons for the way things are. (I'm chuckling as I revise this paragraph. God led me to write many months ago what I need to read today as I lie on a

---

* John White, *The Tower of Geburah* (Downers Grove, Ill.: Inter-Varsity Press, 1978), p. 315.

hospital bed seven hundred miles from home. Here in California to lead a retreat, I suffered an intussuscepted intestine and had emergency surgery to remove fifteen inches of it. Sometimes it is *necessary* simply to rest in what is happening today and not worry about the future—or about understanding the reasons for the way things are!)

Blessedness is indeed promised to those who seek the Lord, but the key lies in the seeking. That means to study and pray, to search and wait—even to be tested, to struggle and suffer. Such disciplines of mind and spirit are often hard to engage in when we are feeling lonely. In those times especially we are invited to cling to this promise: "Those who seek the Lord lack no good thing." In believing that statement is truth we find the contentment to accept whatever blessings are or are not in our lives.

"Happiness is not having all I want, but in wanting what I have." Unless our wants are refined by seeking the Lord as David urges, our wants are probably larger than our needs. On the other hand, when the Lord meets our needs, then we can learn to say with Paul, "I have learned in whatever state I am, to be content" (Phil. 4:11b, rsv). Then we will know the Joy we spoke of in Chapter 12.

This chapter has moved through a surprising progression. We began with the acknowledgment that Yahweh enables us to know his goodness in tangible ways. Here at the end, however, we have learned not to depend on what we feel. We can taste and see how good God is, but true maturity of faith will recognize his love even though from a human perspective we might lack good things. That kind of maturity grows as we continue to seek him. Not in the power of a lion, but in the waiting of a saint, we know the fullness of blessedness.

FOR FURTHER MEDITATION

1. How can we taste God's goodness?
2. Do I receive God's love best through hearing about it, reading about it, or feeling it in a hug?
3. What is blessedness?
4. What does it mean to me that I am a saint?

5. Have I ever thought that I lacked anything? What have I thought I lacked? How do I feel about that after studying this text? (Don't worry if this text still upsets you—it takes time for us to learn such difficult principles as this one.)
6. How do I see others trying to meet their needs in "lion" ways?
7. How does it affect my desires to know this promise from Yahweh: that if I continue seeking him I will never lack any good thing for my life?

16. The Lord Is Near When We've Lost All Hope

Come, my children, listen to me;
  I will teach you the fear of the Lord. . . .
The righteous cry out, and the Lord hears them;
  he delivers them from all their troubles.
The Lord is close to the brokenhearted
  and saves those who are crushed in spirit.
A righteous man may have many troubles,
  but the Lord delivers him from them all.

Psalm 34:11, 17–19

Surely it was the saddest day of my life. Marguerite had listened to me many times through the pain of my husband's leaving. She had given me a plaque that said, "I'm your friend, no matter what," so I went to her home to sit in her rocker and cry. I didn't expect to be able to find any comfort.

When I arrived, she got out her Good News Bible and read to me the eighteenth verse of Psalm 34. "This verse is just for you," she said:

The Lord is near to the brokenhearted
  and saves those who have lost all hope.

I had lost all hope of ever being able to face life again—even to smile again, much less to deal with this terrible pain. All I knew was the despair of rejection, desertion, poor health, and betrayal. Why go on?

Marguerite helped me to find the courage for that day. It was here: "The Lord is near to . . . those who have lost all hope." I couldn't feel his presence. I didn't know any of his answers. I wouldn't have my marriage restored. But I did believe that he was near.

It is still hard for me, even tonight, to write about that pain, but maybe you are feeling such despair right now. Or perhaps you have felt that way in the past, or you will need to know where this chapter is for someday when you will comfort a friend or family member suffering grief or depression. We need to find in the depths of despair a basis for hope.

Tonight it is also hard to write about this because so many of my friends and family are going through such pain right now. Nancy is battling leukemia; Tim, who must endure kidney dialysis, is having terrible complications from the flu. Six of my close friends are unemployed, and several members of my family are going through traumatic times of decision and difficult circumstances. Where is there hope in the midst of all this pain?

The New English Bible translates the first phrase of verse 18 "The LORD is close to those whose courage is broken." The original Hebrew could signify the brokenness of the will or courage, but "broken of heart" in the Old Testament more often refers to one's moral character, in the sense that God searches and refines the heart. In that case, the phrase would mean that Yahweh is near to those who are crushed by their own sinfulness and guilt.

Another scene in *The Tower of Geburah* illustrates well this concept that the LORD remains close even when we are appalled by our failures. The girl Lisa has been deceived by the evil sorcerer and has feasted upon all sorts of delicacies that were not real food. Then she tried to clean herself up in a shower of water that was not real. When she finally meets Gaal, the Shepherd, she is filthy and sticky and afraid that he won't want to touch her. Yet he takes her hand gently. Even when she wipes her dirty hand on his sleeve, he does not pull away. In fact, his robe remains white, and some of the stickiness is removed from her hand.

The nearness of the LORD to the brokenhearted implies the same tenderness. No matter how dirty our face, how dark our shame, how troubled our spirit because we have spoiled our relationship with the Shepherd, yet he still chooses to be beside us in our grief.

Much of the sorrow of the brokenhearted takes the form of those terrible questions "Why?" or "What could I have done?" Our brokenheartedness is often multiplied by the intense guilt we feel (usually falsely). In the LORD's nearness we can learn more truly what is sin—for which we are freely forgiven—and what is false guilt—which he will help us put away. Thus, the Apostle Paul begins and ends many of his letters with a reminder of that forgiveness and that release when he wishes his readers, "Grace to you and peace."

In the poetic parallel line to "The LORD is close to the brokenhearted," David declares that Yahweh saves or delivers those who are crushed of spirit. The verb is from the root *Yashah*, from which we get *Yeshua*, the Hebrew word for our English name *Jesus*. This meaning of the name is noted when the angel says to Joseph, "You are to give him the name Jesus, because he will save his people from their sins" (Matt. 1:21).

We who are New Testament people know, then, *how* Yahweh saves those who are crushed in spirit. No matter how shattered we are by our experience, he has accomplished that deliverance through Yeshua, the Saving One.

"Crushed in spirit," may be interpreted in several ways. It is often understood as "contrite in moral character." In that case, the salvation promised in this psalm is the gift of forgiveness and eternal life for those who are repentant. However, we might also understand the phrase more in the sense of being shattered or crushed emotionally—or, as in the Good News Bible, to have lost all hope. It is probably in our most despairing times that we identify with this interpretation.

Whatever the interpretation, this message is the same: Yahweh is near and Yahweh rescues. This is the hope to which I clung in the many months when all I could do was cling. When I felt so crushed that I didn't feel capable of holding on any longer, my pastor would reassure me, "Don't forget, Marva. God will never let you go." In the midst of the blackness of despair, we need to keep hearing the word of comfort that he is near, until we can believe it and see its true light.

The poet David is realistic. He continues by acknowledging, "A righteous man may have many troubles." The alliteration of the Hebrew words *raboth* ("many") and *ra'oth* ("troubles") underscores our reaction of panic or despair to the multiplicity of our problems. Thus, the fact that we have so many problems gives us one more. Many are the miseries or distresses of the righteous—the ones who desire to be just and good. We who choose God's ways set ourselves up for extra trials—not because we deserve them, but because, when Satan is losing us, he has to fight harder to try to destroy us.

Consequently, we can rejoice when we encounter struggles in our spiritual lives. They prove that we must be doing something right if the powers of evil have to work so hard to try to stop us.

I don't mean that flippantly at all. We must realistically face the corollary between growth in faith and an increase in troubles. Several years ago, the members of some discipleship groups that I was leading ran into all kinds of obstructions as they tried to establish habits of Bible study and prayer. One person kept oversleeping and losing the time she wanted for prayer and meditation. Another started running into irritations in her job that distracted her when she tried to study the Bible. A third complained that his mind always wandered when he tried to concentrate on prayer. Others noted family problems, mechanical breakdowns, crazy frustrations. As we talked about the various difficulties we were encountering, we realized that they were not merely human struggles. The "powers of this dark world" and "the spiritual forces of evil in the heavenly realms" (Eph. 6:12) don't like it at all when we are serving God and extending his principles in the world.

According to C. S. Lewis, there are two mistakes we can make about Satan. One is not to take him seriously enough. We must pay attention to the realism of such phrases as "many are the afflictions of the righteous" (King James Version). The other mistake is to take him too seriously and fail to remember that in his death Christ defeated him once and for all. The Easter empty tomb is the seal of that victory. Therefore, we can assert with the poet that, though there are many troubles for the righteous, "The LORD delivers him from them all" (v. 19). This same verb for "delivers" is used earlier (v. 17), when David declares that when the righteous cry out Yahweh hears them and delivers them from all their troubles. In the Hebrew, repetition and parallel use proclaim these words doubly to enfold us more richly in their comfort.

The verb *to deliver* comes from a root that means "to snatch away," so it connotes the idea of rescuing us from the midst of those troubles. That verb choice is important, because sometimes our circumstances cannot be changed. If someone deserts us, God will not cram his will down that person's throat and force him or her to come back. Nevertheless, in the pain of that rejection, Yahweh comes near to those who are his and takes them away from that grief. We must be patient with the long process of healing, yet we can be confident that ultimately the LORD delivers us from our straits and distresses.

Because I wait for healing impatiently, I included verse 11 in this chapter's discussion. This invitation comforts us softly: "Come, my children, listen to me; I will teach you the fear of the LORD." Many times in my deepest pain I long for the security of being a child crawling into my daddy's lap and feeling his arms around me while he gives me the wisdom to solve all my problems. David certainly had plenty of experience in knowing the LORD's deliverance from his troubles; consequently, he can tenderly address his listeners as children to invite us to learn from him.

I think the text further invites us to learn from all those whose greater years with the LORD have given them deeper wisdom. We gain hope by learning from those who have suffered the same griefs we bear. They can teach us how they survived them, how they have grown from them, and how Yahweh was near in the midst of them. That is the great value of biographies and testimonies of faith.

What distinguishes good biographies and testimonies from bad ones, however, is the subject of the second line of this verse. David says, "I will teach you the fear of the LORD." We are not helped by human words of comfort or pride in human achievements. We are given lasting comfort and eternal hope in whatever enables us to honor Yahweh better and to turn to him—expecting that he will deliver us and believing that he knows what he is doing.

As I look back upon the times of deepest pain and grief, I realize that I was more helped by those who said, "Things are going to be tough for a while, but God is with you," than by those who patted me on the back glibly with, "Everything will turn out fine." The first words might sound cruel, yet I remember rejoicing at their truth.

Just a few weeks ago, a very wise counselor admonished me

to die to my own desires in order to pursue my ministry. He encouraged me to face realistically the fact that my work as a freelance Bible teacher might necessitate a solitary life, so that I can be available to travel anywhere to teach. He analyzed my lifestyle and needs and concluded that it would be very difficult to find anyone to share them. My experience in dating confirms the accuracy of his insights. Even though these hard words meant pain, they were the best words I've heard, because they forced me to confront the truth.

Similarly, we are here reminded that we need to listen to instruction that will help us learn to fear the LORD. That reality will truly help us deal with our brokenheartedness, because in honoring him we will discover that he is near. In fact, he is nearest in our broken repentance. When we are crushed—by our sin or by our circumstances—then we know most deeply that he comes to love.

FOR FURTHER MEDITATION

1. How might my insights into these verses enable me to minister to a friend who is brokenhearted?
2. Why is it comforting to know that the LORD is near when I am brokenhearted?
3. What does it mean that the LORD saves?
4. Am I comforted by knowing that the troubles afflicting the righteous are many? Why, or why not?
5. How can I cope when Yahweh does not seem to be delivering me out of my troubles?
6. Who are my heroes of faith, those to whom I listen for words of wisdom and instruction?
7. Why is it important that they teach me how to fear the LORD?

17. I Thought I Would Die, But the LORD Helped

Who will rise up for me against the wicked?
Who will take a stand for me against evildoers?
Unless the LORD had given me help,
I would soon have dwelt in the silence of death.
When I said, "My foot is slipping,"
your love, O LORD, supported me.
When anxiety was great within me,
your consolation brought joy to my soul.
Psalm 94:16–19

The whole day I had been anxious. Every dimension of my life seemed unsure and troubled. Several options had fallen through for how I could use my big, five-bedroom house for ministry. A nasty letter had come from someone I had been counseling, and I felt angry that after I had invested so much time my intentions had been so misunderstood. Also, troubling news had come from my publisher about the manuscript of my second book. Finally, I couldn't handle it all and called Tim for help. Often when he is on kidney dialysis runs, I call him and we talk about matters of ministry and personal concerns. Tim is a church youth worker and musician and just a few years older than I. A skilled counselor, he really understands the struggles of my physical limitations as well as the hardships and joys of ministry, so he has helped me through many difficult times and questions.

But it wasn't a day for a dialysis run, and Tim wasn't home. I left a message for him to call, but he didn't—now I knew God had abandoned me and didn't care. I went to bed still uneasy and fitful.

Soon the phone rang. My friend had returned and, since I'm usually up late at night to write, had decided to call me in spite of the hour.

I hadn't been rejected after all! As I poured out my troubles one by one, Tim kept rebuking me gently, helping to put things back into the perspective of God's love and care. I told him all the difficulties about my house, and he answered, "Is it God's house or isn't it?"

He was right. I had bought the large house in order to have enough room to welcome into my home those who needed care. Now that the director of our crisis ministry had gone back to school, I couldn't care for guests along with my traveling and writing. Surely God would help us find another way to use his house to minister to the needs of others. Tim's question made me feel ashamed that I doubted so much God's concern for all *my* concerns.

I told him of my anxiety about my book, and he replied, "Did you put that book into God's hands or didn't you?" His words of rebuke came out of such a loving spirit that I wasn't offended. If I write books to share the answers of the Scriptures, surely I must know that the God of those Scriptures will take care of those books. Tim's admonition turned me back to the comforting character of our God.

The surprise came when we had finished talking about struggles, and he didn't hang up. We talked into the wee hours of the morning—in uplifting ways and about pleasant things, so that I was not only comforted but delighted. That conversation had changed a painful and fearful loneliness into a deep security in receiving God's gifts of comfort and love.

When I first studied them, the four verses from Psalm 94 at the head of this chapter struck me with the same wondrous progression that I have just described. This psalm calls upon God to avenge the poet on his enemies, who are jubilant and arrogant. The writer is upset: Troubles are crushing Yahweh's people, yet God doesn't seem to be paying attention.

In the twentieth century, we are probably not oppressed by people in the same way as Israel was in the time of the Psalms. Life is much more subtle now. People oppress us through business manipulations, indifference, exploitation, and institutional injustice, so we are not as aware that they are enemies. Therefore, when we look at this psalm through modern eyes, we must apply it to the enemies that our culture produces: stress, economic chaos, insecurity, anxiety about our own power or prestige, and so forth.

When these things attack us, we cry out with the poet, "Who will rise up for me against the wicked? Who will take a stand for me against evildoers?" Our frustration grows because no one seems to be on our side. On the day I described in the story, nothing seemed to go my way—as if *my* way were best! At one point in our conversation I complained about the struggle that life has been for me for so long, and Tim asked gently, "Is that really what this year has been like?"

His question shamed me, because this year I have experienced more hope than in the last six. Yet at times when too many irritations pile up, it is easy to feel that no one is on our side.

Into our questions comes a resounding answer, "unless the LORD had given me help." His assistance enabled the poet—and me—to find an escape and go on. The word *help* is the same Hebrew noun that is used in Psalm 46, where the poet declares, "God is our refuge and strength, an ever present help in trouble." I discovered him to be such a help through the person of my friend Tim.

The poet records in Psalm 94 how deep his fear and anxiety were. Unless the LORD had given him help, "I would soon have dwelt in the silence of death." The word translated "soon" in the NIV is a Hebrew phrase that means "nearly" or "almost." Without Yahweh, he would almost have settled down in silence. Though the word *death* does not appear in the Hebrew text, it seems to be implied, and that matches our experience. In times of despair we think we are almost going to die.

Perhaps this rising terror at whatever we might be confronting is one of the most critical causes and effects of loneliness; the terror both comes from our loneliness and increases it. When pain seems to overwhelm us with its crushing waves and no one takes a stand for us against the evil, then we panic. If God doesn't do something drastic, we will surely die.

The psalmist has recorded his anxiety to encourage us; someone else has felt so great a terror and has overcome it. We dare not treat lightly another person's panic or depression. The horror of evil rising up against us is very real, and a person being overwhelmed does indeed feel alone and defenseless.

However, the poet goes on to describe how mistaken he was. "If I said, 'My foot has slipped,' your *chesedh*, Yahweh, will support me." In Chapter 1 we learned that the LORD's *chesedh* connotes a depth of loving-kindness unmatched in the world's love. When we feel we are slipping over the edge, Yahweh's steadfast care will support our deepest being. On my day of panic, the affirmation and love my friend Tim proclaimed to me were from the LORD.

I was still loved, even when I was fitful and complaining. This is what supports us best in our moments of pain and panic: the assurance that we are loved even though we are doubtful people. If we can know that we are cared about when we feel rotten about ourselves and our fears, then we can have the courage to change and not be afraid. The loving-kindness of Yahweh is what we need to hold us when we feel we are slipping. Then we will realize that it is a false conception, for we are really being cared for tenderly by our LORD.

The last verse contains the surprise. Not only does the loving-kindness of Yahweh support us, but furthermore, it actually brings us past the point of panic into a sense of well-being that can even bring delight.

Even though our anxieties multiply, still the LORD's love can lead us beyond them. The original Hebrew text says, literally, "in the abundance of my disquieting thoughts in my inward parts." That thorough phrase graphically illustrates the depth of anxiousness that afflicts us at times. Disquieting thoughts or uneasy doubts seem always to multiply, not just arithmetically, but geometrically. Furthermore, they don't just afflict us on the surface, but they attack us in our deepest recesses, where they are harder to handle.

Our "inward parts" may literally be attacked: I think, for example, of one night when I received bad news about a friend who was very ill. I thought I was taking it all in stride and handling the anxiety reasonably well, until I began to have serious digestive malfunctions. The tension was much deeper than I could be aware of on a conscious level.

We are troubled more and more deeply, and the disquieting

worries seem to multiply. However, into that reality thrusts this other: the consolations of Yahweh.

The word that the NIV translates "consolation" is actually plural in the Hebrew. It comes from the verb root meaning "to comfort or to console, to have compassion upon someone." Used always in a plural that intensifies, the noun depicts profound soothing.

The consolations of Yahweh, the poet declares, take the soul to the point of delight. This verb *to delight* is in a continuing tense in the Hebrew and comes from a verb meaning "to sport." It is used in Psalm 119:10, where the poet delights in Yahweh's *torah*, or instruction. It is also used in Isaiah 66:12 to picture a child being dandled upon the knees of a doting parent. The soul, signifying the seat of emotions or passions and, especially here, the place of Joy, is figuratively dandled upon the knees of Yahweh in his consolations.

Not only does God bring us comfort, but he brings us such an abundance of it that we are led out of the state of fear or anxiety that was plaguing us and beyond it into sheer delight.

One of the best ways for me to picture that movement from despair to ecstasy is in terms of music. If I am discouraged, I play a favorite classical record and, in listening, find myself transported beyond myself into a new realm of light and exhilaration. Much of this book has been typed to the accompaniment of the stirring music of Rachmaninoff.

What kinds of things uplift you like that? Do you ever pause to consider that those gifts to you are the consolations of Yahweh, meant to bring you out of anxiety into a celebration of delight? What a loving LORD we have, furthermore, that he gives his gifts to us according to our pesonalities.

When I first moved into this big old house to use it for a crisis ministry, I became very discouraged at how much a stranger I seemed. I felt ripped away from all that had been my security, especially when a new wife took my place in my old home.

In that sense of being lost, I wondered who would "take a stand for me." Like the poet I felt at times that if it were not for the LORD giving me help, I surely would have dwelt in the silence of death. But Yahweh continues to give his gifts of consolations.

I shall never forget the first night that I felt at home in this place. Finally, my office was ready in the basement. My books had been unpacked at last and put in order in new bookcases. My typing desk filled the alcove, the wood stove had been checked, and the husband of one of my friends had connected my stereo.

Late in the evening, I lit the fire, made a pot of tea, turned on a favorite symphony, and sat in my rocker. At first I didn't even notice, but suddenly I was supremely aware that I'd come "home." I rocked and cried with delight in the goodness of the LORD that, at last, I felt I belonged somewhere.

It isn't the room. It is the place created by the LORD to bring me his consolations. They don't merely comfort me: They remind me of his surprising love, which lifts us beyond our troubles to heights of Joy.

FOR FURTHER MEDITATION

1. At what times in my life have I felt that there was no one to stand up for me against evil?
2. When has the evil been so overwhelming that I wanted to die—or thought I would?
3. In those times, how have I known the help of my LORD? How have I seen his *chesedh* in action in my life?
4. How have I misperceived my circumstances and thought I was slipping when actually the LORD was supporting me?
5. How have I experienced the multiplication of anxieties deep within me?
6. How have the consolations of the LORD brought me, not only out of anxiety, but also into delight?
7. How might I help someone who is anxious to find the delight of Yahweh's consolations?

18. The Wicked Aren't So Fat and Sleek

Surely God is good to Israel,
  to those who are pure in heart.
But as for me, my feet had almost slipped;
  I had nearly lost my foothold.
For I envied the arrogant
  when I saw the prosperity of the wicked.
They have no struggles;
  their bodies are healthy and strong.
They are free from the burdens common to man;
  they are not plagued by human ills. . . .
Surely in vain have I kept my heart pure;
  in vain have I washed my hands in innocence. . . .
When I tried to understand all this,
  it was oppressive to me
till I entered the sanctuary of God;
  then I understood their final destiny.

Psalm 73:1–5, 13, 16–17

The young man wept in my office. "It isn't fair," he cried. "Everything is going just fine for her. She's running around, having a lot of fun. And I'm in misery."

He had been on the verge of suicide because he doubted the justice of God. Psalm 73 surprised him with its intensely practical application to our everyday lives.

We have all felt at times like the psalmist Asaph does. We don't know very much about Asaph other than that his name heads several psalms. Nevertheless, he certainly has keen insight into human experience. He understands with deep wisdom the tremendous pain suffered by those who watch the ungodly have it all. This just doesn't seem fair: Those who try to stay pure suffer more than those who don't care.

Just like the psalmist, we rant and rail against the injustices of life. There had better be a good answer, or we won't be able to believe that God is really a good God.

Because we get ourselves into such a state of mind, the poet begins with a statement of faith: "Surely God is good to Israel, to those who are pure in heart." Later he will question whether or not it is worth the effort to keep one's heart pure, so he begins by asserting that it is and then wrestles through to belief in the truth of that statement. The process is instructive when the inequities of pain and suffering cause us to doubt.

The psalm itself begins with the word *surely*. The poet announces this thesis at the outset: God is indeed good to Israel, to those who are clean in heart (which refers to their moral character). Purity is worthwhile after all, he proclaims, but then continues, as if to say, "But let me tell you how I almost forgot."

In fact, he humbly admits, "As for me, my feet had almost slipped; I had nearly lost my foothold, for I envied the arrogant when I saw the prosperity of the wicked." That simple reality almost undid him and his faith. His spiritual feet tripped over the confusion in his mind.

We envy the ease of the arrogant in their sin. Last weekend a couple having an affair talked with me about how much they care for each other and how important it is to express that love. Their evident happiness belies the belief that if we participate in sexual relationships outside of marriage we will ultimately not be as fulfilled as if we continue to follow God's moral principles. In our loneliness, we envy the freedom of the wicked to sin. Life would be much easier if we could just have an affair and not feel so guilty about it.

If we still choose God's principles, we must battle not only our loneliness, but also the peer pressure of our sexually loose culture. We wonder why the others all have lovers, but we don't have anyone to hold us. Who will respect our struggle to stay pure?

"They have no struggles," Asaph declares. They don't seem to suffer spiritually or physically. "Their bodies are healthy and strong." In literal Hebrew, this description of the well-being of the wicked is cryptic: "For not the pangs. But fat their body." Not only do they not suffer from the bonds and fetters, but also their bodies are well provided for. In fact, they are fat. The word the NIV translates "body" actually is the one for "belly," from a word meaning "in front of." Therefore, literally, the expression says that their belly is prominently fat. One can't help but notice how well off they are.

Why do so many of my friends struggle with severe handicaps—Tim with kidney failure and Linden with paralysis and Nancy with leukemia—when the "wicked" seem to be "free from the burdens common to man"? "They are not plagued by human ills." Of the troubles or labors of ordinary people, there is nought for them. Contrary to what most people experience, they are not stricken. The last participle in the Hebrew comes from a verb meaning "to touch or strike" and is usually associated with diseases. They seem to escape the touch of pain. Why? The result is that "pride is their necklace" (v. 6).

No wonder that after several more verses describing their pride and scorn and mockery of God, the poet summarizes his frustration in these words: "This is what the wicked are like—always carefree, they increase in wealth." Such disparity is more than we can take.

So the poet complains. "Surely in vain have I kept my heart pure; in vain have I washed my hands in innocence." The latter might imply ceremonial washings, and thus we might infer, "It really does no good to be faithful about matters of worship, either."

The poet is terribly disgusted that he hasn't benefited from trying to be God's person. The Living Bible captures his attitude well with this rendering: "Have I been wasting my time? Why take the trouble to be pure?" (v. 13). To have expended such effort has been emptiness, he pouts. The "heart" of the first phrase and the "hands" of the second line remind us in poetic parallel that both the inside and the outside have been kept clean—but to no avail, it seems.

The poet doesn't want to speak about it publicly; that would upset the crowds. However, when he tries within himself to understand, everything is oppressive to him. The sorrow, the vexation, the pain of labor hadn't produced results. The more one tries to understand injustice, the more grievous it becomes. The Hebrew calls it "travail."

Repeatedly, what gets our faith into trouble is the attempt to understand. We keep asking, "Don't they know they have sinned? How can they not feel any sorrow that they have hurt me so badly?"

The more we try to understand and make things somehow fair, the more oppressive it becomes to us. Envy of another's well-being, even if it was achieved by sin, can never be constructive. There must be a better way to deal with the pain of it all.

The poet knows a better way. After much vexation, he takes a wiser course. Verse 17 begins with a rare construction in the Hebrew to mark a decisive turning point, "until." Things were oppressive as long as the poet was trying to understand with his own mind; the bitterness could be changed only by his going to the sanctuary of God.

Actually, the Hebrew word is plural and says, "sanctuaries," which might designate the temple and its many precincts about the Holy of Holies. Signifying many sacred places, the word is more easily transposed into our times. We need not necessarily go to a church somewhere to get our minds straight about the inequities of suffering. We can enter any sanctuary. The word comes from the root *qadosh*, or "holy," and thus can refer to any holy place.

I paused just now to put lotion on my fingers and to rest them because they are cracked. What an irony to have them bleed as I write this chapter about envy of those whose bodies are healthy and strong and who seem to have everything in life going for them. Yet, when I enter the sanctuary of this writing corner, I wouldn't trade places for anything. Here in this holy place, God and I are the only ones up.

I'm sure you have some special sanctuaries, too. When you go to those places (even if just in mind and not physically), there your searching intellect and troubled heart can find rest. In the sanctuary places we meet with God to learn his answers to our probings. Indeed, only his answers will suffice. We will never be able to explain satisfactorily such problems as the breaking of covenant marriage relationships, the limitations of physical handicaps, or accidents of freakish nature. We can't completely calm the agony in our minds by coming to grips with reality or gaining insight into it. Nevertheless, in the sanctuaries there are answers of another sort.

The poet says, "Then I understood their final destiny." The Hebrew verb in that clause means "to give heed to, to consider with great attention." When the poet enters the holy place, he puts all things into an eternal perspective, and that makes a huge difference in how we view life—and death—and life again.

We will look at the conclusions he comes to more closely in the next chapter, but here at least we note the different perspective. Always life seems unfair until it is put into the whole picture of forever. We who believe in Jesus Christ already possess eternal life. It is not just "pie in the sky in the by and by when we die." The verbs in John 3:36a ("Whoever believes in the Son has eternal life") are present tense verbs. If we already have that gift, then we must understand how it will affect our view of things now.

The Apostle Paul writes to the Ephesians that "God raised us up with Christ and seated us with him in the heavenly realms in Christ Jesus" (Eph. 2:6). This insight means that we no longer view things only with human eyes, but we share Christ's mind and seek his view of things in the light of God's power active on our behalf.

Having an eternal perspective does not simply mean that we look forward to heaven when all this pain will be over or that we are glad because the wicked who seem to prosper now will really suffer in hell. In fact, the prospect of the latter increases our concern for them and motivates us to try to invite them into a relationship with God, too. Rather, having an eternal perspective means that we learn to recognize that the pains of this life are not all that there is to reality.

I think, for example, of how much more I appreciate friends now than I did before I went through the agonies of the last five years. Our capacity for happiness seems to be greatly enlarged by the depths of sorrow through which we pass. Eternity enters into our appreciation of our relationships with friends now.

When we again consider the end of the wicked, we see that they, too, to some extent are experiencing it now. Though they appear to be fat and happy, deep inside a longing in them cannot be quenched. Sometimes they have to work terribly hard to hide that restlessness from themselves, and sometimes they seem to succeed. But where there is sin, there will also be guilt and sorrow and emptiness. Cruelty works its own rewards, and evil bears its consequences. Therefore, seeking revenge does us no good. Rather, our frustrations can enable us to grow in our eternal perspective. To that growth we will turn in the next chapter.

FOR FURTHER MEDITATION

1. Can I assert with the psalmist that God is surely good to those who are pure in heart?
2. What experiences in my life have caused me to doubt that assertion?
3. Have I observed that the wicked seem to have no problems? How does that make me feel?
4. How do I deal with my own envy of their supposed well-being, or with the pain that their hurting me has caused?
5. Why is is oppressive when we try to understand these apparent injustices?
6. What are some of the sanctuary places in my life?
7. How does an eternal perspective affect my view?

19. In Our Brutishness, God Holds Our Hand

> When my heart was grieved
>   and my spirit embittered,
> I was senseless and ignorant;
>   I was a brute beast before you.
> Yet I am always with you;
>   you hold me by my right hand.
> You guide me with your counsel.
>   *Psalm 73:21–24a*

Today as I swam a long training workout, I experimented with counting by praying for ten different subjects on a repeated cycle. On the first lap I prayed for my housemate, who is still unemployed, and on others, for those who are ill and for my family. On the sixth lap I sprinted thanksgivings, and each tenth was filled with praise.

Repeating that sequence for three hundred laps, I kept realizing the immaturity of my faith life. When I envy the wicked, I have forgotten how rich life with God is.

The poet's graphic picture of his previous ingratitude and poor attitude is something with which we can all identify. At times we have all reacted much as Asaph did to the prosperity of those who hurt us.

The first verb in the Hebrew text is a form of the root that means "to be sour or leavened." In the intensive reflexive (Hithpael) form this word means "to be embittered." The poet says that his heart, here denoting the seat of his emotions, was embittered when he saw the inequities that we considered in the last chapter.

Next, in the poetic parallel, Asaph confesses that in his kidneys he was pierced. The noun *kidneys,* used as a synonym for the word *heart,* also implies in the Old Testament the involvement of one's character; consequently, the word is used to describe the object of God's examinations. Thus, when the poet acknowledges that in his kidneys he was pierced, he realizes that God, too, searches and knows him.

His poignant envy had pierced him. We must admit that we cause much of our own pain. Truly, some pain comes to us from the outside, when others hurt or reject us; however, we multiply it many times by our envy and our untrusting spirits. To accentuate the sharp piercing that his own envy had caused him, the poet uses a form of the verb root that means "to whet or sharpen." The Jerusalem Bible illustrates with this graphic translation: "When my heart had been growing sourer with pains shooting through my loins."

Beyond what was happening inside himself, the poet also realizes that his comparisons and attitudes affected his outward behavior. Verse 22 begins in the Hebrew with an emphatic pronoun, which seems to say, "But I *myself*—how terrible that this is how I was." There is no verb in the original text, which says, literally, "I—brutish!" so the predicate adjective stands out more disparagingly. The word *brutish* (translated as "senseless" in the NIV) is related to the noun for "beasts" and the verb "to be stupid or dull-hearted." In the Scriptures it describes the one whose spiritual sensitivities are too dull to perceive truth.

The NIV translates with the adjective *ignorant* the Hebrew phrase "and I do not know." The Jerusalem Bible captures well the sense of this phrase with its rendition "I had simply failed to understand." The result of such failure, the poet continues, is that he became a behemoth—that is, a brute beast or a hippopotamus—in his relationship with Yahweh.

Like a hippopotamus—not a very lovely picture for describing oneself, but we identify with it very closely. Sometimes we are shocked at how brutish and blundering and ignorant we have been, how we have not trusted when so much evidence points to the LORD's trustworthiness. The Living Bible grasps this whole sequence well in this paraphrase: "When I saw this, what turmoil filled my heart! I saw myself so stupid and so ignorant. I must seem like an animal to you, O God." I want to add, "because I seem so much an animal to myself." The Jerusalem Bible says, "My stupid attitude to you was brutish."

A necessary part of our spiritual growth is to see ourselves

this way. We've got to face up to the senselessness of our lack of
trust so that we can see, with Joy and wonder, the infinite surprise that God should love us anyway, in spite of our ignorance
and brutishness.

That surprise is captured well in the Living Bible. Right after
saying, "I must seem like an animal to you, O God," the paraphrase continues, "But even so, you love me! You are holding
my right hand!"

After all the brutishness on our part, we are shocked that
God should love us anyway. The original Hebrew again begins
with an emphatic pronoun to say, "But I myself—greatly to the
contrary of what I might have expected—continually with
you." Again, the absence of a verb accentuates with precise
terseness, "I continually with you."

It is not an illusion. With you continually I myself *am*.

It is not an on-again, off-again deal. I am with you *continually*.

It is the relationship that matters above all. Continually I am
with you.

The word for "continually" (or "always" in the NIV) is actually a noun meaning "continuity" that is used in significant
places, especially in the Psalms and in the Book of Isaiah, as an
adverb. One of my favorite places is this eighth verse from
Psalm 16: "I have set the LORD continually before me. Because
he is at my right hand, I will not be shaken." (That verse is
especially related to our study here because of the reference to
the right hand, which is held by Yahweh in Psalm 73.) We also
saw this noun used as an adverb in Psalm 34:1, where David
declares that the praise of Yahweh will "always be on my lips."
(See Chapter 13.)

The always-ness of our relationship with the LORD takes us
away from our brutishness into the freedom of acceptance.
Too easily we might take that continuity for granted or even
think that we justly deserve God's love. A good hard look at the
beastliness of our ignorance is a necessary dose of strong medicine.

To say that we are with Yahweh emphasizes that we are in his
thought and care, as we have observed in other chapters of this
book. But in this verse an unusual fact surfaces. The pronoun
that is attached to the preposition *with* in the Hebrew is the

feminine singular *you*. In other words, the LORD is addressed here as a woman. The feminine pronoun was also used in the previous verse in its connection to the Hebrew preposition *with* to declare that the poet became a behemoth "with you." But in verses 24 and 25 the pronouns shift back to the masculine form.

These passages are made more poignant when we think of God as feminine. To be brutish and ignorant and like a hippopotamus before a feminine softness and gentleness sounds more ugly and crass. To be in wonder at the love of a feminine God sounds more enfolding. One of the strongest words for "love" in the Old Testament is a word that comes from the root meaning "womb" (see p. 26), so we are invited throughout the Scriptures to think of God's love and compassion in motherly terms. Thus, the wonder and surprise multiply, for when we have been beastly senseless, the LORD still directs his maternal care toward us. He still holds us as special children in relationship with himself.

The contrast is also strong between the feminine relationship of our being continually with the LORD and the masculine grasping of our right hand that concludes verse 23. The verb I translated "grasping" means "to take hold or to take possession," but it is used here in a gracious sense rather than in a manipulative or exploitative sense. Yet it is a word of power. God does take us firmly by the hand in spite of our brutishness in order to pour out upon us his gifts.

The right hand among Semitic peoples was always significantly the sign of goodwill. Thus, Jesus speaks about sitting at the Father's right hand (Luke 22:69), and the Apostle Paul exults because Peter and the other apostles extended to him the right hand of fellowship (Gal. 2:9). That action connoted acceptance and empowerment.

To reach for someone's left hand was a put-down. By contrast, verse 23 underscores the gladness. The phrase literally says, "the hand, my right one." Because of the pun on "right" in English, we can see more deeply that God knows what he is doing in choosing to care for us even though we have been hippopotamuses: He holds our hands—the right ones.

Again, the fantasy *The Tower of Geburah* provides an illustra-

tion. When the Shepherd takes her hand in spite of its stickiness, Lisa is overwhelmed with gratitude. How could he love
me in such a state as this?

That wonder fills us, too, as we meditate upon these verses
and relate them to our loneliness. Sometimes in the pain of
being alone, we are aghast at the terrible brutishness, the ignorance, of our lives. We didn't notice things or said the wrong
things. We messed everything up or can't seem to get things
right. Yet in the midst of feeling like a hippo, we can hear this
glorious assertion: "Yet I am always with you; you hold me by
my right hand." We remember that the "you" refers to Yahweh in both his masculinity and feminity and realize that all of
God's character is fully available to us in our relationship. In
our next chapter, we will see further the results of this new
awareness on the part of the poet—and for us.

First, however, we need the reminder that Yahweh wants to
guide us with his counsel (v. 24a). He is always with us and takes
us by the hand so that we don't make such stupid mistakes so
often.

In the context of the whole psalm, we need the guidance of
the LORD to enable us to perceive truly the difference between
the outcomes for the wicked and for ourselves. We need his
guidance to learn to be grateful for the ways things develop
and to look to him for their development so that his purposes
can be accomplished.

Yahweh's instruction is our greatest need. Many years ago
my life was revolutionized by a professor who pointed out to
me how God had answered my prayers in ways I had not observed. Since then, I have been amazed by the frequency of my
failure to perceive God's will. He wants to lead us in beneficial
ways, but we often panic before we recognize his guidance, and
then we try to find things on our own.

That is exactly what had happened to Asaph to make him
embittered about the prosperity of the wicked. When he focused his attention upon them, rather than upon Yahweh, he
was overwhelmed by the inequity of things. However, if our
focus is upon the LORD and his purposes, we are so busy being
faithful to our own calling that we don't have time to worry
about the fortunes of others; nor do we have the space to be

envious, because we are so filled with the enjoyment of our own
ministries and God's gifts in our lives.

Many verses in the Psalms speak of God's faithfulness in
guiding his people—such as Psalms 23:3; 31:4; 43:5, and
139:10. Our problem often lies in not realizing that Yahweh's
counsel comes to us in many different forms—through the
Scriptures and books about them, through the wisdom of
friends and counselors, through opportunities that develop and
those that don't materialize, through our own insights gained
in devotional meditation.

We need to believe that God wants us to know his will, so that
we can be released from that terrible panic of trying to find it.
That is why the psalmist makes this bold declaration: "You
guide me with your counsel." Truly, when we pay attention to
the LORD's instruction, we will not behave as hippopotamuses.
We will not turn sour; we will recognize Yahweh's guidance for
our lives as part of the Joy of his continual presence.

FOR FURTHER MEDITATION

1. How have I seen my own spirit turn sour in response to
   circumstances around me?
2. In what situations has envy pierced my kidneys?
3. In what manifestations have I seen and been ashamed of my
   own brutishness? In what ways do I (spiritually) resemble a
   hippo?
4. How do I know that I am continually with Yahweh?
5. Why does Yahweh want to stick with me when I am brutish?
6. How have I seen in my life that he has grasped me? How
   have I seen that he has taken my right hand to accept me
   and to grant me his gifts?
7. How have I experienced the counsel of the LORD? What
   means does he usually use to guide me?

20. To Desire Nothing on Earth

> . . . and afterward you will take me into glory.
> Whom have I in heaven but you?
>   And being with you, I desire nothing on earth.
> My flesh and my heart may fail,
>   but God is the strength of my heart
>   and my portion forever.
>
> *Psalm 73:24b–26*

On the far edge of the huge store were the grand pianos, and while my friends were pricing organs I was free to putter. Giving up on the touch of a nine-foot grand, I tried a seven-foot-four-inch August Forster piano from Germany. Its touch was exactly balanced; its tone, lusciously rich; its workmanship, finely crafted. What delicate candlelight and raging fire the keys could pull from the heart of the strings! The salesman urged me to compare it with all the other pianos in the store.

There was no comparison. Nothing could match the thrill of playing that August Forster.

Once we know the LORD of the heavens and gain a heavenly perspective, how can we desire anything less on earth?

Two definite movements compose Asaph's final response to his former ignorance in questioning the prosperity of the wicked. First, as we saw in the last chapter, he recognized his brutishness and knew that Yahweh was yet with him to guide him and gift him in this life. Furthermore, he recognized that there is a wholly (and holy) other dimension to our existence and to our relationship with the LORD.

Scholars debate whether or not the poet is thinking about eternal life in the second half of verse 24. The phrase "and afterward you will take me into glory" is an unusual statement for a Hebrew writer. The Old Testament does not contain much of a concept of life after death. Only in rare places, such as Psalm 16:11 and Job 19:25–27, do we catch intimations of immortality. Consequently, by the time of Jesus, controversy reigned between the Pharisees and the Sadducees, those who believed in life after death and those who didn't. The religious leaders tried to cast Jesus into the midst of that controversy on some occasions (see, for example, Luke 20:27–40), and the Apostle Paul makes use of it in his self-defense (see Acts 23:6–11).

If Asaph is referring to eternal life here (which is very likely), then he is greatly ahead of his time. He could also be referring to the future in an earthly sense. In that case, he would mean that after his bitterness about the wicked had gone, and after God had guided him out of whatever had caused him so much grief, then he would assuredly experience Yahweh's glory. As the Living Bible notes, the Hebrew phrase could be translated "afterwards you will bring me unto honor." If this interpretation is correct, then the poet is speaking about securing justice in this life.

It seems to me more probable that Asaph is looking to life after justice has been fully restored at the end of time. However, as applied to modern times, the point must be that the eternal life to which we look forward will determine our attitudes toward this life now. A heavenly perspective must affect our desires and our confidence, where we put our trust.

The Hebrew word *glory* means also "honor or dignity of position or abundance." Because the concept involves all these things, we have to see the word in this text with its eschatological ramifications. Eschatology is a study of the last times, when we will experience the ultimate fulfillment of all God's promises to us. In our life of faith we realize that the heaven to which we look forward is also experienced to some extent, but not fully, now. We call it "realized eschatology" when we experience the Joy of heaven in this time and space.

Because we look forward to the glory that someday will be our entire and permanent, eternal possession, we discover that *now* we are elevated to positions of dignity and abundance and honor in the sight of God. If we believe, Jesus tells us in John 3:36, we receive the gifts of eternal life now.

Thus, this text invites us into tasting the delights of heaven, even though some of its best gifts are yet to come. How much better it will be when we are fully taken into glory, without any vestiges of pain or sorrow.

After all, the poet continues, whom do we have in heaven but Yahweh? He is the only LORD of all.

Elementary school studies about Greek and Roman mythology made me think about the difficulty of living under such a system. Whenever troubles came, how could one figure out which god was mad now and how to appease him or her without getting any of the other gods upset?

Going to a Lutheran school, I thought already then how liberating it is to have only one God! Now even more that truth brings comfort. As we have been seeing throughout our study of Psalms together, whenever we learn to know better the character of our God, then we grow in trusting Yahweh and in receiving his *chesedh* or steadfast love for us. The fact that there is no competing deity enables us to enjoy the comfort of God thoroughly. We do not live under a dualistic system, wherein the powers of evil have as much control as those of good. Because Yahweh alone is God, nothing can thwart his plans. If we have him alone in the heavens, we therefore know some particular things about our struggles on earth.

The first thing that follows is this perspective: "And being with you, I desire nothing on earth." Having the LORD of all lords to be our God, would we ever again settle for anything less? Even the magnificent August Forster cannot begin to produce music such as his.

To choose discipleship necessitates some hard wrestling, however, because many times we do settle for less. The verses from Psalm 73 bring us back to a balanced (and godly) perspective on the things of this world. Sometimes we think we can't get along without a certain possession or a certain person or a certain kind of comfort. To feel that way is to make idols out of whatever we desire. I am horrified by the diversity and frequency and intensity of my idolatries.

Our deepest spiritual longing is to be able to say with Asaph, "and being with you, I desire nothing on earth." Necessarily, then, our idolatrous human desires must be killed, but our own rebellious nature oftentimes prevents this. Don't misunderstand this point: Human desires themselves, such as the longing for someone's love, are not wrong. What makes them wrong for each of us is our elevating them to the place of God so that we want the satisfaction of our desires more than we want him.

What things distort our perspectives? An article in *Sojourners* magazine connects our idolatries to the teaching of Jesus in this way:

The point is that we are prone to make gods of the secondary realities we know and love—marriage, family, money, and possessions. We want to substitute them for radical dependence on God.

Jesus is calling those who follow him to live by an ethic of relinquishment: relinquishment of old crutches and identity-creating relationships in order to live totally abandoned to the will of God. . . .

The key question raised for each of us in Jesus' teaching is: What is the major obstacle that prevents us from following? Is it our money, our loved ones, our vocation, our self or community image that we need to maintain? What is behind all of these? Does our pride prevent us from trusting God? Our insecurity, our need for love, our fear of discomfort, suffering, and death?*

Our text from the Psalms reminds us that these secondary realities are not really worthwhile compared to our relationship with God, whom alone we have in the heavens.

That point is underscored by the fact that, after all, our bodies are wasting away. Verse 26 concludes that even though our flesh and heart might waste away, yet our relationship with God will not. The verb for "wasting away" speaks of being spent or used up, to be exhausted, or to fail and, thus, of the ephemerality of our days and vital strength. (Compare chapters 6 to 8 of my first book, *To Walk and Not Faint.*) The word *flesh* signifies the physical power or the external apparatus of a person, as opposed to the heart, which denotes the inner self. Both inner and outer will surely fade away. All flesh is grass, the voice cries in Isaiah 40:6, 8. In fact, we experience this world's death every day.

In a clever play on words, the poet again uses the word *heart* to say that the gifts of the LORD will last forever when he is, literally, "the rock of my heart." When our inner person is focused on the LORD as its support and defense, then his might and grace keep us forever. The word for "rock," translated "strength" in the NIV above, is used thirty-five times in the Old Testament as a figure for God. Surely the people in the Holy Land recognized the permanence of rocks, especially in contrast to the shifting sands, which are blown around by the desolate winds of the wilderness countryside. Rock stands silhouetted against the sky as a symbol of permanence.

---

*Jackie Sabath, "Euclid Street Journal: A Wedding Sermon," *Sojourners,* vol. 10, no. 11 (November 1981), p. 25.

Though my heart might fail, Asaph says, the rock of my heart will endure. Moreover, he is also my "portion." This is the word that is used in Psalm 16:5 to emphasize that Yahweh has given his people "a delightful inheritance." There the poet declares, "LORD, you have assigned me my portion and my cup; you have made my lot secure."

Here in Psalm 73 the LORD himself is the portion. Even more than the gifts that he pours out upon his people, the LORD himself is actually the possession of his servants. How thoroughly we can know his intimate presence!

The phrase is a good summary of everything in this section of the psalm. The very God who alone resides in the heavens as LORD over the universe deigns to let his people possess him. He gives himself to those who believe in him and desire him above all else.

We can't possess him if we don't desire him. If we make anything on earth a god in his place, then we miss out on the gifts available to us, both now and in the future.

Such an eternal perspective is our hope against the inequities of time and sorrow. When the wicked seem to be prospering while we continue to suffer in serving the LORD, we are assured that our desire to remain pure is not a waste of time, but a movement toward, and to some extent a participation in, the genuine fulfillment of our deepest longings.

FOR FURTHER MEDITATION

1. What do I think the phrase "glory afterward" refers to?
2. What does it mean to have an eschatological perspective?
3. How does having an eschatological perspective increase my Joy now?
4. What does it mean to be taken to glory?
5. What things do I make into idols here on earth?
6. What does it mean to me that Yahweh is the rock of my heart?
7. What does it mean to me that he is my portion?

21. Even in Death the LORD Protects Us

The cords of death entangled me,
    the anguish of the grave came upon me;
    I was overcome by trouble and sorrow.
Then I called on the name of the LORD:
    "O LORD, save me!"
The LORD is gracious and righteous;
    our God is full of compassion.
The LORD protects the simplehearted;
    when I was in great need, he saved me.
Be at rest once more, O my soul,
    for the LORD has been good to you . . . .
Precious in the sight of the LORD
    is the death of his saints.
                                    Psalm 116:3–7, 15

My friend Nancy called this afternoon from a hospital in Seattle. Her cold had developed into pneumonia, and she was about to go into surgery for some cauterization to stop hemorrhaging. Her many-years' struggle against leukemia seems to have reached its final weeks.

When Nancy first called to ask for prayers, a blood clot on the brain was causing severe seizures, but she had only a 30 percent chance of surviving any surgery to remove it. What is the place of God's comfort in the Psalms for the loneliness brought by severe illness or imminent death?

The loneliness of the hospital seems to me the toughest thing about terminal illness. Friends can't be as supportive there, limited as they are by visiting hours, kept distant by sterile precautions. A few bright cards or drooping flowers cannot give a bare-walled room the warmth of home. Unfamiliar nurses and procedures, frightening machines and injections, and foreboding symptoms make the dying person feel alien to all that is living.

Perhaps that is your loneliness right now or perhaps you

know someone who is struggling with it. Perhaps you have just recently lost your beloved one in death. Psalm 116 offers particular comfort for dying saints and for those who stand beside them—or without them.

Actually, of course, we are all dying, but for some of us the process is going faster than for others. Actually, also, we believers are all saints already. We don't have to wait till our deaths to receive that title. By his declaration of forgiveness, we were immediately made saints when we first knew the LORD as our God. Since then he has been refining us to make us into the saints that we are. These facts must have an effect upon our dying.

A friend once asked Nancy, "How can you counsel others about death when you yourself are dying?"

Nancy replied, "I'm not dying. I know where I'm going."

The friend protested, "Don't give me all that heaven stuff."

Nancy answered, "I'm not giving you all that heaven stuff. I just know that I'm going home to be with my Father." Nancy's confidence has made her battle against leukemia a remarkable testimony by which others have been profoundly touched with the reality of the love of God.

That is the Joy. Yet we must also acknowledge the pain and the loneliness of dying. The psalmist expresses well one element of its agony when he says, "The cords of death entangled me." For someone caught in terminal illness the grip of death is an inescapable reality.

"The anguish of the grave came upon me." This second line in the Hebrew says, literally, "The straits of Sheol befell me." "The straits" signifies the worst possible distress, even that of the underworld Sheol, the dark abyss to which the Old Testament people thought they would go after death and not be able to return. No wonder the poet was experiencing great "trouble and sorrow." The first noun pictures adversity, whereas the second speaks of grief and mourning.

These two graphic word pictures sadly motivate us to pay more attention to easing the struggles of those in anguish. Indeed, the pain of suffering is terribly intensified by the fact that one has to bear it alone. No one else can do our dying for us. No one can really understand the fears and doubts that go through our minds and spirits.

Notice, however, that the poet responds to this anguish of soul and body by calling on the name of the LORD. The second line of verse 4 uses in the Hebrew a strong particle of entreaty that introduces this phrase: "Ah, now, Yahweh, let my soul slip away." The verb could also be translated, "be delivered." We don't have common English idiomatic expressions that give the thrust of the opening particle. The word means "please," but very much intensified. More so than at any other point in our lives, the time of our death is a time for strong calling to the LORD with all the pain and anguish of our being. Now more than ever we will be helped by being honest with God about our feelings.

Nancy has been an example of being real with God in her prayers as she pours out to him all the feelings of her pain and discouragement. She knows she's not perfect; she knows her own stubbornness—so she is very real about being real.

But from this, Nancy can genuinely assert with the poet, "The LORD is gracious and righteous; our God is full of compassion." The word *gracious* is used in the Old Testament primarily as a description for an attribute of God. He is uniquely gracious in a way that no human could ever be, and that graciousness includes the fact that he declares us to be saints. Any graciousness in us comes in response to his.

Notice how this term is used in the following passages from the Psalms: "But you, O Lord, are a compassionate and gracious God, slow to anger, abounding in love and faithfulness" (86:15). "The LORD is compassionate and gracious, slow to anger, abounding in love" (103:8). The context of each of these verses includes a description of how God's graciousness is evidenced in the lives of men and women who are his saints.

Furthermore, the poet in Psalm 116 says that Yahweh is righteous. What he does is eminently just. We might question how his love can allow such evils as leukemia or heart disease, paralyzing accidents or kidney failure. Yet, ultimately, his righteousness can be seen in light of his graciousness and his compassion, the third attribute of the trio. The latter is again the word that comes from the Hebrew root for "womb" so it stresses the maternal love and tenderness of the LORD. Because of that intense love and the unique fullness of his graciousness, we can trust that what is righteous is also ultimately good.

Because these three characteristics mark his relationship with us, the next verse is even more comforting. The poet declares that "the LORD protects the simplehearted." The Hebrew verb is one that means "to watch over in order to preserve or to keep safe," so it brings to mind an image of enfolding. The Hebrew text is especially comforting because the verb is used in the form of a participle, which stresses its continuing action. God doesn't just protect once in a while, but constantly, indefatigably, he guards his saints. If you are on a hospital bed, he is watching over your intravenous needles and blood transfusions, your respirators and heart pacers. He is more constant than the nurses to keep you in his care. When I have been deathly ill, that deep sense of his presence has been for me a strongly comforting assurance.

I prefer the New American Standard rendering of the adjective in verse six as "simple" rather than "simplehearted" (NIV). The original Hebrew does not limit the simpleness to the heart, so perhaps it could refer to those who are simple of mind, in the sense of being open to the instruction of wisdom. Perhaps "the simple" could denote those whose simplicity of faith keeps them trusting in any circumstances. That kind of faith can declare with the poet, "When I was in great need he saved me."

Surely, to believe that Yahweh still saves requires a simplicity of faith when one is suffering excruciating pain, battling against overwhelming odds, or agonizing in suffocating loneliness. Sometimes the LORD saves by delivering unto death, but then his salvation is experienced most fully. The important point is to recognize his saving action in whatever takes place in one's life—or death.

When a person who is dying can wrestle through to that kind of assurance, then that person can truthfully make the next statement with the poet, "Be at rest once more, O my soul, for the LORD has been good to you."

When I was a senior in college, emotional trauma severely upset my insulin balance. Long hours of spiritual struggle finally brought me to the point of knowing the LORD's protection and graciousness, and then, at last, I could be at rest. Believing in the LORD's goodness, I was ready to trust him for whatever direction he might choose to take my life at that point. I was even a bit disappointed when I didn't die, for I really felt as Paul did when he wrote, "I desire to depart and be with Christ, which is better by far" (Phil. 1:23).

Remembering the LORD's character strengthens our faith to say that. Our lack of simpleness convinces us that we must understand everything before we can accept all the facets of our lives. The LORD's protection is more apparent to those who simply trust without all sorts of obstructing rebellion.

The Hebrew text of Psalm 116's seventh verse says, literally, "Turn back, my soul, to your rest, for Yahweh has benefited upon you." The state of rest described implies a security that is vitally connected to the assurance that the LORD has benefited a person. If we know that Yahweh has been, is now, and will continue to be good to us, we can rest securely in that gracious hand.

More than anything, people in our confused and tumultuous society long for security. We who are Christians can look forward to our death, for when we leave this life of sorrow and pain and go home to our Father, as Nancy says, then we will finally know a perfect security. Furthermore, in looking forward to that unmarred rest we are able to rest securely now. "I know where I'm going, and I know who's going with me," the song says. In the LORD's company we have assurance for the meantime.

Probably the most comforting message of all is the fifteenth verse of Psalm 116, wherein the poet declares, "Precious in the sight of the LORD is the death of his saints." The poet lived through whatever ordeal he was experiencing to write about Yahweh's answer to his prayers and the deliverance he received. In his case this verse means that his death was so precious to the LORD that he delivered him out of it. (I must add, several months after the first writing of this chapter, that Nancy, too, was delivered from her fight with death and, to the surprise of everyone, has experienced a complete remission. We who prayed fervently for God's healing in her life are filled with wonder at the miracle we are observing.)

When applied to us, this fifteenth verse has larger meanings. Our death is so precious to the Father that he gave up his Son to take away its sting for us. Through the death of Jesus, eternal life has been made available to the saints. Therefore, we know that our deaths are highly valued by the LORD; they mark our entrance into the fullness of his kingdom. He cares intensely about every death because his desire is for "all men to be saved and to come to a knowledge of the truth" (1 Tim. 2:4).

Furthermore, our deaths are precious to him because of the very dying itself—even if it might be a terribly painful death. He knows and cares, and, though we can't understand his wisdom, he can bring good things even from the greatest afflictions (Rom. 8:28). When everything hurts, when we face the terror of leaving our loved ones, it is hard to remember that our God's character is marked by the infinite graciousness, righteousness, and compassion that we have discovered in this chapter. He wants us to believe that these traits are his, even in the midst of our pain and suffering. Only then we can be comforted by such words as those of Paul to the Romans that the sufferings of this present time are not worth comparing to the glory that is to be revealed in us (Rom. 8:18). Or we can look to other promises and be assured that for those who endure there is indeed a crown of life (see, for example, 2 Tim. 4:6–8 or Rev. 2:8–11).

The preciousness is our comfort. We are helped by knowing that every concern in our dying matters infinitely to God—so much so that he will even use our dying as a means for drawing others to himself. How gloriously God has used Nancy's courage and love in the face of death to make others curious about her faith. Frequently, Nancy has been able and ready to give an answer to those who ask her for an account of the hope that lies within her (1 Pet. 3:15). Moreover, that hope has been so evident in her dying that those of us around her have all been strengthened to see God's faithfulness at work.

We have also been encouraged by seeing how the LORD has used us to minister to her in the tough times of her struggle. Truly we have all been deepened by this process. God's purposes are good beyond our understanding. Certainly he won't let such a corrupted thing as death interrupt them. When Nancy's struggle against leukemia is finally won (maybe years from now), when the LORD delivers her from those cords of death, then his purposes for her will be most fully complete. In that victory we will all rejoice at his compassion, even as we mourn the loss of her. Then she will know a perfect rest as the Father welcomes her home. God himself will tell her how precious her death has been to him.

FOR FURTHER MEDITATION

1. How can I bring comfort to those suffering the anguish of aloneness in dying?
2. How can I prepare for my own dying?
3. Am I really with God in my prayers? Do I make strong entreaties to him?
4. What is the force of the combination of the three attributes by which God is described in verse 5?
5. Why is it that the simple are more able to receive the comfort and assurance of the LORD's protection?
6. Why am I able to turn back to rest when I know that Yahweh has been good to me?
7. Why is it comforting to me to know that my death is precious in the eyes of the LORD?

22. Lest We Forget That We Are Special

For you created my inmost being;
   you knit me together in my mother's womb.
I praise you because I am fearfully and wonderfully made;
   your works are wonderful,
   I know that full well.
My frame was not hidden from you
   when I was made in the secret place.
When I was woven together in the depths of the earth,
   your eyes saw my unformed body.
All the days ordained for me
   were written in your book
   before one of them came to be.
How precious to me are your thoughts, O God!
   How vast is the sum of them!
Were I to count them,
   they would outnumber the grains of sand.
When I awake,
   I am still with you.

Psalm 139:13–18

Despite all the emphasis these days on "human potential," most of the assertions of unique individuality sound hollow. Sometimes the voice proclaiming a person's importance sounds so strident that we think with Shakespeare, "He doth protest too much." Who is trying to convince whom?

Lack of self-esteem especially afflicts those who are lonely. If we have been rejected, or we feel as though we have never been accepted, we can't convince ourselves that we really are unique human beings with much to offer the world around us. We need texts like Psalm 139 to tell us objectively why we are so special.

Our importance is not determined by our own efforts; our Creator made us special because he is. Theoretically, we who know that should have no problem with our self-identity. Unfortunately, often our faith doesn't penetrate to our bad feelings about ourselves. In the struggle to like ourselves, we need again and again to listen to the Scriptures, like the promise in Romans 8 that nothing can separate us from the love of God or like these verses from Psalm 139 that show us how that love was at work in creating us specially.

Anyone who doesn't know the Creator cannot appreciate the intricacies of his creation. Unless we trust the Designer we can't rejoice fully in the wonder of his plan.

The setting of these words of encouragement is a wisdom psalm that recounts the greatness of God in terms of his omnipresence, omniscience, omnipotence, and omni-judgment—the fact that he is everywhere present, all-knowing, all-powerful, and perfect in his judgments. The mood of the psalm is one of wonder that the poet can be in a relationship with this God who is so "all" about everything. That relationship is the foundation for our worth and significance.

The very first line of this section of the psalm underscores our specialness. The Hebrew text says, literally, "For you created my kidneys." The word *kidneys* is used to signify the most sensitive and vital part of a person. Figuratively, then, it refers to the seat of the emotions and affections and, therefore, includes the character of a person. Thus, the Jerusalem Bible translates the word with the phrase "inmost self," and the NIV says, "my inmost being." A modern paraphrase might be, "the true me." The phrase, consequently, offers this great comfort: When our loneliness is intensified because no one seems to know our true selves, God understands every facet. After all, he put us together.

Indeed, we are known by God (1 Cor. 8:3). When God originated our complex personhood, he designed us with special kidneys—that is, the special sensitivities and attributes that compose our inmost self. His plan is good; he said so. The truth of his declaration sets us free to accept our uniquenesses, too.

The second picture is equally compelling, for its verb, *wove*, implies great care and craftsmanship. The poetic parallel asserts, "You wove me together in the womb of my mother." God didn't just throw us together; he carefully chose all the threads and then wove them together into the beautiful patterns that you and I are. No two tapestries are ever alike, so we see personal tenderness and love in the weaving. The Lord chose for each of us uniquely the perfect combination of the color of hair and eyes and skin, the level of intelligence, the various aspects of personality and gifts, the abilities and weaknesses and strengths.

The poet responds to this wondrous creation by vowing, "I praise you because I am fearfully and wonderfully made." The verb *to praise* is often used ritually to signify formal worship, but it is also used throughout the Psalms to declare personal thanks or adoration. The two adverbs in this line are especially graphic. *Fearfully* comes from the verb *to fear* and is used to describe wonderful or glorious things that are so awe-inspiring that they cause astonishment. In other words, we are amazed by the wonder of our creation—not with the fear of terror, but with the fear of reverence and honor.

The form of the second adverb, translated "wonderfully," stresses the accomplishment of something that is surpassing or extraordinary. In other places, its verb root signifies that which is beyond a person's power to understand. The word comes from the root for "wonder." The extraordinariness of our creation is vastly beyond our comprehension.

We become more aware of the magnificence of human creation when we see how one organ's malfunctioning has so many adverse effects on other parts of the body. The failure of my pancreas in my teen years made it impossible for me to gain weight, to metabolize food effectively, to develop properly. Now the intricacies of balancing blood sugar with activity and insulin affect my gum tissues, vision, the speed of healing, the sensitivity of the fine nervous system, the ability of my body to increase blood pressure to handle energy needs, and on and on. How could these interconnections have happened by accident?

The statistical probability of even one protein molecule being formed by random chance is too incredibly low to be possible. Even if we constructed a small protein molecule of twelve different amino acids, its chain could be fashioned in 1×10^{300} ways. If we had just one example of each of these possibilities, they would weigh 1×10^{280} grams—which is enough protein to fill the entire known universe (since the earth itself weighs only 1×10^{27} grams)! Such facts boggle the mind and make us wonder how anyone could doubt God's hand in forming the right molecules for our existence.

The poet seems to recognize the danger of skepticism, for he

continues, "Your works are wonderful; I know that full well."
As if he were reminding himself not to take the glory of it all
for granted, he says, "Yes, LORD, I am amazed by your works. I
really recognize how magnificent they are."

The word *wonderful* echoes "wonderfully made" (v. 14a), so
once again we are reminded that God's creation exceeds our
ability to comprehend. Yet we can know exceedingly well that
God is the performer of these works.

The verb *to know* is in a form that pictures a state of being,
the constant action of knowing. We just can't forget how wondrous his works are once we get to know them (and him).

The final word in the Hebrew text of this verse ("full well,"
NIV) is one that is often translated "exceedingly." It comes from
a root meaning "to turn or surround" and implies a great abundance. This is the same word used in the last verse of Genesis 1,
where God looks at all that he has made, including mankind
which was created on that final day, and says not merely that it was
good, as he had said on the previous five days, but that it was
"good exceedingly." In response, then, the poet of this psalm
knows "exceedingly" that the works of the LORD are wonderful.

Next, the poet rejoices that when he was created in the secret
place (probably again referring to his mother's womb), his frame
of bones was not hidden from the LORD. He saw, in fact, the
embryo, the unformed substance. This statement is seen by the
pro-life movement as a good argument from a Christian perspective against abortion. If indeed God is part of the whole process of
creating life and putting together the embryo, then it is murder to
cut off that life before its process of formation can be completed.

Of course, the poet was not addressing the issue of abortion.
Nevertheless, his rejoicing over God's knowledge and action in
the process of human development must cause us to think more
thoroughly about that subject ourselves.

The verb *to be woven together* actually connotes great skill. It
comes from a verb root that means "to variegate" and implies,
therefore, the variegated cloth that workers in colors weave. It
recalls the image of being woven from verse 13 and brings to
mind the same ideas of care and craftsmanship we encountered
there. The "depths of the earth" is figurative for the dark and
hidden interior of the womb, where God skillfully does his

work to make the individual person. Certainly we must see how special we are that from the moment of our conception God was putting us together as lovingly as a many-colored tapestry.

Next, the poet exults that in the LORD's book all of his days that were pre-ordained were written down before any one of them yet existed. We must keep this critical concept clear of distortions. Our lives are not pre-fated so that we have no choice in them at all. That misconception is precluded by the tense of the verb *to write down*, which here signifies an incompleted action. God is writing them, but we have a chance to choose what he writes. Nevertheless, they are "pre-ordained." This verb is in the perfect (completed action) tense and in the intensive passive (Pual) form of a root that means "to form or fashion." This particular form of the verb *to pre-ordain* stresses that God's purpose is to establish the days in a certain way.

We must put these two concepts together carefully to understand their paradox a bit better. God has a basic plan for our lives, but he will not cram it down our throats. If we choose his plan, things will be best. Yet we have the free will not to choose it, and then, because he loves us so much, he will still work things around for our benefit (Rom. 8:28). We won't have his best, but he will make whatever we choose into the best possible.

This paradox sets us free from any fatalistic notions about our lives, yet it gives us the sweet comfort that God really does have a design for us. I think about that often because I love my work so much. When I'm right in the middle of teaching about the Scriptures, I sometimes think, "This is what I was made for!" What Joy we find when we live out the LORD's design for our lives, especially because he doesn't force us to choose it. If we are obedient to his perfect plans, we will find the deepest fulfillment.

That is why the poet continues by declaring how precious God's thoughts have become to him. He realizes how vast is the sum of them. The Hebrew word translated "sum" comes from the root for "head or chief" and might signify that which is the best or the choicest. Altogether God's thoughts are precious, and each is precious because it is best. God's designs and purposes become the deepest desires of our hearts. They are precious to us because we want to be right in the middle of them.

The final picture in this section is one of my favorites in the

Scriptures—especially because of its humor. The poet says,
"Were I to count them, they would outnumber the grains of
sand," and then suddenly he adds, "When I awake, I am still
with you." That is a terrific way to handle insomnia. He got so
involved in counting all the thoughts of God that he fell asleep.

This final line also offers vast comfort: "When I awake, I am
still with you." We can never fall out of God's thought and
care. Even though we fall asleep, the LORD never will. We are
again and again, repeatedly, furthermore, besides, yet, still,
moreover, enfolded in his mind and heart. As Jesus says, no
one can snatch us out of the Father's hand (John 10:29). We
don't really know very many of the thoughts of Yahweh, but
this one we know for sure: He will always love us. Nothing can
separate us from his love—not even our falling asleep when we
count his graciousnesses. Truly this picture of ourselves, mar-
velously designed, made with his tender care, should fill us with
dignity and self-worth. We don't have to win God's approval;
we had it even before we were born. We don't have to prove
our worth; he wove it together. We don't have to impress him
with our goodness; he just wants to show us his.

FOR FURTHER MEDITATION

1. How does it make me feel to know that God really knows my
   inmost being?
2. How does it make me feel to think about God weaving me
   together?
3. What parts of the human creation most fill me with wonder?
4. Do I know exceedingly well the wonderful works of Yahweh? Why or why not?
5. How does it make me feel to think that God has ordained all
   my days? How can I reconcile the paradox of his preordina-
   tion and my free will?
6. How do I feel about the abortion issue after studying this
   text?
7. Why does it comfort me to know that when I fall asleep over
   trying to count God's goodnesses, I am still with him?

23. Help to Resist Temptation

O LORD, I call to you; come quickly to me.
  Hear my voice when I call to you.
May my prayer be set before you like incense;
  may the lifting up of my hands be like the evening sacrifice.
Set a guard over my mouth, O LORD;
  keep watch over the door of my lips.
Let not my heart be drawn to what is evil,
  to take part in wicked deeds
with men who are evildoers;
  let me not eat of their delicacies.
Let a righteous man strike me—it is a kindness;
  let him rebuke me—it is oil on my head.
  My head will not refuse it.
Yet my prayer is ever against the deeds of evildoers;

Psalm 141:1–5

The struggle against being lonely is itself compounded by, and in its turn complicates, the problems of facing temptations. Longing to be held and loved, we can more quickly meet our needs by immoral means. Or perhaps we are tempted to over-eat and abuse our bodies. Unfortunately, we can too easily drown the sorrow of our loneliness and satisfy our cravings (but only temporarily) by giving in to our sensual appetites. We may be driven to alcohol or drugs in a hopeless attempt to drown out the pain.

Sometimes those temptations become overwhelming, and we feel, "What's the use?" Life is so miserable that we think we can vastly improve it if we give in to whatever temptation is oppressing us. Especially if we have been married, the desire is incredibly strong in us, not only to satisfy our sexual needs, but also to prove to ourselves and to the world and perhaps to the former spouse that we are sexually attractive.

So how can we find the resources for fighting the seemingly insurmountable odds against us in the battles against tempta-tion? I especially find helpful Paul's words to the Ephesians in chapter 6, where he lists the armor that we are to put on to defend us against Satan's attacks. Prayer is greatly emphasized as the most essential tool for the fight, as it is here in Psalm 141. Both the beginning and the end of the section that we will discuss focus on prayer as our greatest weapon.

Another major emphasis in this psalm, which Paul doesn't stress in Ephesians, though he does talk about it in other places, is the support and rebuke of fellow believers. In the Christian body we are strengthened to combat the temptations that besiege us.

As a child participating in evening vespers, I always loved the liturgical sequence in which the pastor said, "Let my prayer be set before thee as incense," and the congregation responded with the chant, "And the lifting up of my hands as the evening sacrifice." At the time I didn't know what those lines from Psalm 141 meant, especially because in Lutheran churches we don't usually lift up our hands in prayer, but I was stirred by the dramatic action in them and sensed that they involved a plea for relationship with God.

The Hebrew word translated "set" is one based on a root meaning "to fix or establish." In the form used in this verse it means "to arrange or set in order" so that as incense the prayers might present themselves before the LORD. I have never liked the smell of incense very much, so I have to adjust that image in my mind to remember that for God it is a pleasing aroma, a fragrance that is special. We are asking with the poet David that our prayer be a sweet smoke of sacrifice before the LORD. We want the lifting of our hands in prayer and praise to come to him even as the grain offering was brought as a tribute in the evening time of worship.

The gesture of raising hands in prayer illustrates the nature of our relationship with God and puts us into proper humility before him—stretching out our hands both to beseech him and to reach for his hand of care. Dramatic fragrances and actions put our prayer life into perspective. Though we join the poet in asking Yahweh to come quickly, we also want to have proper respect and patience in our prayers so that we don't call in ways that are demanding and don't acknowledge who we are before him.

Perhaps the poet feared that his speech might be improper before the LORD. Wanting all the words of his prayers to be righteous, he adds, "Set a guard over my mouth and keep watch over the door of my lips." Similarly, we don't want anything to violate our prayer life, to be irreverent, or to come from wrong motives.

Even the form in which the poet makes these requests underscores the reverence with which he speaks. "Set," "keep," and "let" in verse 3 are not simple imperatives, but add what is called a paragogic *hē*. This letter at the end of an imperative makes it softer, as if we were to add the word *please*. Thus, we are asking the LORD to station a guard for us and to watch over our speech *please*. We don't want any dishonoring to come between our LORD and ourselves.

Nor do we want evil to get in the way. The real problem in temptation is not only that it causes us to sin, but that it breaks down the relationship. Consequently, the poet asks that his heart not even be drawn in the direction of that which is evil, because to move in that direction is to go away from the LORD. The word *heart* here must be understood more deeply than the way we use it in English. Here it specifically refers to inclinations, resolutions, and determinations of the will. We don't want our desires or intentions to be drawn to any matter that is ethically wicked or immoral.

This thought prepares us for the words of Jesus that merely to look at a person with lust in one's heart is adultery (Matt. 5:26). Sin is rooted in the intentions, so the place where we want God's action to begin in helping us to fight temptation is at the very core of our being in our basic motives.

Especially in the battle against sexual temptations, our thought life must be purified. We want to not even want what isn't according to God's principles.

When the poet asks that he not be drawn to what is evil, the expression used is unusually forceful in the original text because it first uses a rare Hebrew verb (translated "be drawn"); then the noun immediately following it comes from the same root, in order to doubly emphasize how much the deeds are evil. That verb comes from a root that means "to practice or to busy oneself, to divert oneself in dealing wantonly." The noun that follows signifies "deeds," but it is almost always used to denote those that are wanton. We will see this noun used in a shocking way in Psalm 77 (Chapter 28), where it describes the action of God, whose love is so generous that it seems almost wanton. Literally translated, then, the phrase asks the LORD to keep us from practicing evil practices or doing doings of wantonness.

That strong statement is amplified in the next phrase, which adds the poet's desire that he be kept from taking part in "wicked deeds." This word denotes even violence or crime—in other words, much more overt acts of evil. The poet wants to avoid getting involved in such wicked deeds with men who are habitual "evildoers." The Hebrew text calls them men who are "practicing falsehood," a word that stresses the nothingness or vanity of iniquity because it never truly is what it seems to be. Indeed, we will always discover that the evil to which we are tempted turns out to be hollow.

That last comment gives us more ammunition for our battle against evil. We are more thoroughly equipped to fight sin when we remember that it is never ultimately satisfying. Always its pleasure will turn to dust in our mouths. In the fantasy *The Tower of Geburah*, the little girl Lisa ate and ate of the sorcerer's delicacies, but was always hungry just after eating his empty food.

Even so, the poet David specifically says, "Let me not eat of their delicacies." We might wonder what he is referring to, but one application to our own experience is terribly obvious. Many of us wrestle against the temptation to overeat when we get depressed. The word *delicacies* means "dainties" and comes from the word for "pleasant" or "delightful." It implies something very pleasing on the surface that is poisonous in reality. To eat of the delicacies of evildoers pulls us into their traps. In practical terms, falling to the temptation of overeating precipitates further evils. Abuse causes people to gain weight, which robs them of their self-esteem, which usually causes them to do more overeating. Temptations catch us in those kinds of cycles, which are always terribly destructive.

Consequently, David asks that he be kept from those temptations, and his plea makes the next verse all the more important.

The poet continues by reminding us of a special aid for resisting temptations: the help of friends.

Verse 5 is much more cryptic in the Hebrew and thereby accentuates its point. Literally, the original text reads as follows:

> Will smite me a righteous one—goodness.
> And he will rebuke me—oil of the head.
> Nor shall refuse my head.
> For still also my prayer against their evils.

Because our prayer is still against the temptations of those who work wickedness, David urges us to be grateful when members of the community who are supportive help us to combat them. If someone smites me to correct me, he says, it is a goodness. Notice that the smiting comes from a *righteous* person. If that person is a model to us of what we would like to be, then the discipline is a favor to us, and we appreciate the kindness.

If that same righteous one will rebuke us, in the sense of chiding or correcting, it will be as oil to our heads. This verb *rebuke* comes from a root that means "to judge or decide," "to prove," in the sense of testing. The righteous one who observes us has weighed our behavior against the standard of God's principles and therefore rebukes. Oil in this case is a token of hospitality or a medicament. It brings us cleansing and promotes healing.

Notice that David's response to such correction is simply the phrase that his head will not refuse that kind of oil. The verb means "to hinder or restrain or frustrate." God's purposes are being worked out through the rebukes of godly friends so we would hinder his plan and cleansing in our lives if we refuse it.

Just recently I was criticized for always hugging my Christian friends. My critic thought that a person in my position as a teacher should be more reserved about giving affection. That criticism hurt because I felt it was unjust, but I need to listen to it to make sure that my actions are genuine expressions of Christian love and not manipulations of people to meet my needs.

When godly friends criticize us, we do well to pay attention. They are frequently God's vessels for bringing correction and for rebuilding our lives. Perhaps you might pause awhile to thank God for those members of the body of Christ who have been agents of God's admonition for you.

The rest of this psalm speaks about keeping our eyes fixed on the LORD when the wicked lay out snares for us. Significantly, this last section begins: "Yet my prayer is ever against the deeds of evildoers." I think that means not only that we don't want those deeds to infect our lives, but also that we want to counter-act their power in the world. Perhaps some concern is also implied for those who are working evil. Maybe we can be helpful to them in drawing them away from their wickedness.

How, then, can we face temptation? Our prayer life is the key. Moreover, the rebukes of our godly friends dare not be ignored. Finally, as we grow in our relationship with the LORD, we will more thoroughly know the resources of his care, not only to counteract the evil that would draw us aside, but also to reach out to help others who face temptations, too. More and more, we could become guardians of righteousness bringing goodness and healing oil to the heads of others.

FOR FURTHER MEDITATION

1. How does the dramatic action of the lifting up of the hands help me to focus on the nature of my relationship with the LORD?
2. What is the reason that the state of the heart is so impor-tant?
3. To what kinds of practices by evil persons am I drawn? What sorts of temptations afflict me, especially in my loneli-ness?
4. How does my loneliness increase my susceptibility to temp-tation?
5. How does my church provide support in fighting tempta-tions? How do I wish it did?
6. Am I able to receive the rebuke of my Christian brothers and sisters? Why or why not?
7. What is the state of my own prayer life? In what ways might I deepen it in order to be able to fight temptation more effectively?

24. God Sets the Lonely in Families

Sing to God, sing praise to his name,
　　extol him who rides on the clouds—
his name is the LORD—
　　and rejoice before him.
A father to the fatherless, a defender of widows,
　is God in his holy dwelling.
God sets the lonely in families,
　　he leads forth the prisoners with singing;
　　but the rebellious live in a sun-scorched land. . . .
You are awesome, O God, in your sanctuary;
　　the God of Israel gives power and strength to his people.
Praise be to God!

Psalm 68:4–6, 35

I held my namesake, Joy Marva Fehring, on my lap while I listened to her brother and sister play their instruments in the high school Christmas concert. This afternoon the wonderful music was more than just a concert because I was with my "family," who had made me part of them by asking me to be a godmother for baby Joy.

Earlier in the day in Tacoma I had listened with great delight to two other friends who were guest singers for a worship service. After coming to the adult forum I taught on "Keeping Christ in Christmas," my two spiritual brothers gave me warm goodbye hugs. Several such single friends, male and female, are another kind of family to me.

After my class, also, many congregation members came to thank me for the ten weeks I had been a guest teacher on Isaiah. During those three months together, they had become a church family to me.

Tonight a fourth family was created. My housemate Julie and I became instant aunts to Jess and Hope, whose parents, Eugene and Toni Carson, are planning with us to become a Chris-

tian community together. Suddenly God seems to be providing
the answer to my many prayers about his will for this big old
house. Of course, we will have to struggle together to be a
family in this place. But our love for the LORD is of the same
mind, as is our desire to live in community and to share our
resources. I believe that God is going to knit us into a more
effective ministry through our support and care for one another.

How fascinating the timing of God that on the day I had
planned to work on this chapter about the solitary set into families he should set me into four different kinds so that I could
better understand! What love-surprises God has in store for us,
if we can open our eyes to see them!

Psalm 68 does not fit into any of the typical psalm styles. *The
Layman's Bible Commentary* classifies it as "a collection of songs
and poetic fragments for use in a dramatic procession celebrating the Kingship of God . . . . Each part of the Psalm was pre-
sumably sung in relation to a specific act of the sacred ritual."*
You might want to read through the whole psalm first to get a
feel for the context of the section we will be discussing.

I'm sure you noticed that the psalm celebrates God's provision for his people as one manifestation of his Kingship. The
LORD's dwelling on Mount Zion is also part of the reason for
this celebrative procession, as are the deeds that he performed
when he brought the Israelites out of Egypt and into the Promised Land. In the midst of all these descriptions is this verse
that Paul quotes in Ephesians when he is talking about the gifts
God gives to his church to equip the saints for the work of
ministry: "When you ascended on high, you led captives in
your train; you received gifts from men" (v. 18 and Eph. 4:7).

The psalm's descriptions of the procession itself give us
glimpses of the people's experiences as they worshiped together—with the singers and musicians and the maidens playing tambourines and the various tribes coming in their proper
order in the celebrative throng. This graphic section (vv. 24–
27) sets the tone for our discussion of the LORD setting the

---

*Arnold B. Rhodes, *The Book of Psalms*, vol. 9 of *The Layman's Bible Comme
tary*, ed., Balmer H. Kelly, (Richmond, Va.: John Knox Press, 1960), p. 103.

solitary in families. We feel enfamilied when in our minds we join in the festival procession.

Especially note the way the psalm ends, for the last verse is the grand culmination of the message of the entire festival. I love processions with banners and music in our worship, for then we say in our dramatic actions what can't be said in words—that our God is awesome in his sanctuary. The Hebrew says, literally, that God is "causing astonishment out of your holy place." At the place out of which he speaks and exerts his power (perhaps the temple and its precincts) he continually fills those who observe with reverence and awe.

After all, the second to the last line of the psalm concludes, this is the God who "gives power and strength to his people." An emphatic pronoun is used here to underscore that we know the God of Israel because he deals with his people in this manner. The verb is in a participial form which emphasizes more strongly in Hebrew the continuous bestowing of strength. *Power* refers not only to personal power, but also, in this context, to the power of the people as a whole, as a political and social entity. The word that is translated "strength" by the NIV is a word that is used in a plural form in the Old Testament only here, in order to intensify its message. We might translate "strengths" by "abundant might." God gives us more than enough strength to triumph.

Because his gifts are more than enough, the psalm ends with an exultant "Praise be to God." This is not the same phrase that appears so often in Psalms 111–117 and 146–150, in which the Hebrew text says, "Praise the LORD." Here it means, rather, "Blessed be" God. Because the word is a participle again, it stresses that God is continuously to be blessed. The verb means "to kneel before or to bless another," so the psalmist is declaring that God is so worthy of our adoration that our fitting response to what has been manifested about him is to be in the habit all the time of honoring him.

Now, with the whole context of Psalm 68 in our minds, we can focus particularly on verses 4 to 6. First of all, several different verbs are used in this section to urge the people to praise God. The first invitation is to sing to God, and next we are called to play music to his name, which means to honor the

LORD's character. The verb is related to the word for a "pipe," so it means, literally, "to play on a reed." In other words, we are to praise God not only vocally, but also with our instrumental music. The next verb means actually to lift up, in the sense of casting up a highway, though it is used here to mean "lifting up a song of praise to the one riding through the desert places." The NIV translates the final word in that sentence as "clouds," but includes in a footnote the possibility that it means "*desert.*" The word evokes images of the Exodus because it is often used in the Old Testament to describe the wilderness or the steppes through which the Israelites traveled to come to the Promised Land.

The NIV rendition of the next phrase, "His name is the LORD," only hints at the emphasis of this message. The Hebrew says, literally, "In Yah his name." The nickname *Yah*, which is short for *Yahweh*, is used only in late psalms of praise. The sentence means that "His name consists in Yah." The Hebrew preposition *in* is very important in this instance because it emphasizes that God's "name," which is his character, consists in all the attributes of the LORD, who has revealed himself through history with an infinite love and grace. He is indeed Yah, the Covenant Keeper, who is faithful to his promises to provide for his people.

That is why we are invited to rejoice before him. The Hebrew text does not use either of the two most common words to express rejoicing, but a rarer word that means more "to exult in triumph." The word is akin to the one used by Hannah in her song (1 Sam. 2:1) and is behind the word *rejoice* in Mary's Magnificat (Luke 1:47). (See also 1 Pet. 1:8.) Such a word is more in keeping with the mood of the context. This festival seems to be a victorious kind of procession exulting in the triumph of our God.

That is a significant introduction, then, to the next section, which is the focus of our interest. In such a mood of exultation we remember that our God is "a father to the fatherless" and "a defender of widows." Those who are typically the helpless— the orphans exposed to injury and the widows subject to harsh treatment and oppression—are victoriously cared for by the one who is Father and Defender to them. Once again there is a reference to "God in his holy dwelling," the place of apartness from which he exerts his power on behalf of the helpless.

Next, his holiness is manifested on behalf of the solitary. As the NIV translates this passage, "God sets the lonely in families." Scholars disagree over the best translation of the Hebrew phrase here. Literally, the original text concludes, "in the house." According to the New American Standard Version, God "makes a home for the lonely." For the people in the procession that this psalm celebrates, the phrase might refer to the fact that the LORD had led them into a homeland. They had been exiles and friendless, but now God had given them a home.

The phrase is one of immense comfort, not only to the wandering Israelites, but also for those of us who are alone and isolated. God enfolds those who are lonely and gives us a place of security. As I mentioned at the beginning of the chapter, I experienced today a remarkable enfolding into four kinds of families.

The rest of the sixth verse speaks of God leading forth into prosperity those who are imprisoned, in contrast to those who are rebellious, who live in a sun-scorched or glaring and bare place. The noun for "prosperity," which is translated, "with singing," in the NIV, is plural in the Hebrew for intensification. In these final phrases of the verse, then, we see the immense difference between the afflicted ones, cared for by God's provision, and those who, by rejecting him, miss his gifts.

One of my biggest frustrations with the twentieth-century Church is that we don't live out very well the principles of this psalm's procession. If God would use us to provide for the afflicted ones, we are not doing a very good job. Probably widows and orphans are cared for better in our society than in biblical times, so they don't provide the best images today for the afflicted. In our age perhaps the poet would say, "a father to the children of poverty and a defender of minorities and the disabled."

What does the Church do for the lonely? How have God's people learned to love better so that we might be one of the primary families into which lonely persons are set? More and more as I travel to different churches to teach, I grieve over the lack of concern, evidenced by the small number of single persons participating in the congregations. Consequently, I plead with you to be active, out of your own aloneness, to encourage deeper caring in the Church. Out of the healing that we experience can come a powerful ministry of sensitivity to the needs of others around us who also long to be enfamilied.

All sorts of families might offer us comfort and security or a place of ministry. Physical families can adopt us as extra aunts and uncles. (They need the influence of other Christian adults upon their children as much as we need their companionship.) We can be godparents for children and help to raise them to know the LORD. We might consider more seriously the idea of Christians living together in communities. (As I work on the revisions of this book, I'm excited about all the good things that have been happening since the Carson family joined Julie and me in the EPHESUS Community.) Also, marriage is not necessary for deep relationships with friends of both sexes. Many of my close friends are single men whom I love intensely and affectionately, though not in a romantic way at all. These are some of the kinds of families into which God might set us.

He wants to place us into a home, to enable us to feel secure in our aloneness, to change our loneliness into being enfolded. As a tender Father and righteous Defender he cares for us when we are orphaned or widowed. As Jesus promised, "I will not leave you as orphans; I will come to you" (John 14:18).

FOR FURTHER MEDITATION

1. What is the place of dramatic action in worship services? How can I best get in touch with the awesomeness of God?
2. In what ways does he give me strength and abundant might?
3. How can I sing or make music to extol him in the worship life of my congregation?
4. What is the sense of victory that this psalm entails? How do I experience it?
5. Why is it important that "In Yah" is constituted God's name?
6. Who are "the helpless" in our times?
7. Into what families has the LORD set me?

25. Worship Really Matters

As the deer pants for streams of water,
  so my soul pants for you, O God.
My soul thirsts for God, for the living God.
  When can I go and meet with God? . . .
These things I remember
  as I pour out my soul:
how I used to go with the multitude,
  leading the procession to the house of God,
with shouts of joy and thanksgiving
  among the festive throng.
Why are you downcast, O my soul?
  Why so disturbed within me?
Put your hope in God,
  for I will yet praise him,
  my Savior and my God. . . .
Send forth your light and your truth,
  let them guide me;
let them bring me to your holy mountain,
  to the place where you dwell.
Then will I go to the altar of God,
  to God, my joy and my delight.
I will praise you with the harp,
  O God, my God.
Why are you downcast, O my soul?
  Why so disturbed within me?
Put your hope in God,
  for I will yet praise him,
  my Savior and my God.

Psalm 42:1–2; 43:3–5

The times were filled with anxiety and grief. My home had fallen apart; my life's ministry was beginning to move in new directions; I was unsure of everything. The one bright spot in my life was the opportunity to go to chapel whenever I went down to Western Evangelical Seminary in Portland for work on my Master of Divinity degree. I had deeply loved the chapel services when I was an undergraduate in a Lutheran teachers college, so it was not only the soreness of my circumstances that made me so hungry for worship during my loneliest years. To this day I have a deep craving for more frequent corporate worship.

The Scriptures are a treasure chest from which we can continually take out insights both old and new (see Matt.13:52). We can study a text for one theme and then come back to it another time for an entirely different perspective. Because of the emphasis in Psalms 42 and 43 on the soul's longing for God (which is often obstructed by formalized religion that involves us in all sorts of "religious" activities that prevent us from spending time deepening our personal relationship with God), we might easily overlook the other major theme of corporate worship. That theme is stressed especially in the repeated refrain that occurs in 42:5, 11 and 43:5 and seems to indicate that the two psalms were originally one poem.

You might wonder what all of this has to do with loneliness. Unfortunately, our materialistic and alienated culture hides from us the truth that God created us in his image and designed us to have fellowship with him. The great tearing of sin into the world disrupted our relationship with God and, consequently, with each other. Adam and Eve started blaming each other instead of sharing with each other.

God's image in us, however, is not lost completely by our fall into sin. These two psalms describe in a profound way the huge longing we all have deep inside of us, not only for God himself, but also for intimacy with others who are his people. Notice how often statements in the poem imply corporate worship.

At the outset, the poet compares his desire to that of a hart that longs for streams of water. We must remember that he is writing in the land of Israel, which is mostly terribly dry and sun-scorched. I have a hard time identifying with that since I live in western Washington, where it rains most of the time. We must think ourselves into the blinding desert wilderness of the Middle East in order to imagine the intense longing that the poet describes.

The poetic repetition underscores that intensity. The third line of the psalm announces again that the poet's soul, or the seat of his desires, thirsts, not for just anybody, but for the living God, the one who alone is the vigorous fountain of life.

That longing leads naturally in the poem to the following question: "When can I go and meet with God?" We always wonder when we are going to be able to satisfy our appetites and meet our needs. Children ask, "When are we going to have dinner?" I often ask, "When can I have some ice cream?" since that is my chief vice. This poet begs, "When can I have some worship?"

Today such an unusual question must stop us short. How many people that you know are begging for worship? Most children resist, screaming, "Do we have to go to church?" Much of the weakness that we see in churches results from their failure to offer a vibrant fellowship that would both stir up and satisfy longings for God. Perhaps we should each pause at this point to assess the worship of our congregation. Do we offer a place and a time in which people can come to meet with the living God?

Next, the poet remembers the times that worship has been refreshing and meaningful to him. As he pours out his soul in this time of grief and searching, the memory of worship brings him in touch with his deepest need. Observe carefully his description. First of all, he notes that he went to worship with the multitudes. He might be recalling specific times of pilgrimage when bands of believers traveled together to the temple in Jerusalem to celebrate Jewish holidays. The point is that part of the Joy of the worship was being together with many others who were believers, too.

Secondly, the poet was one of the leaders. He was an active participant in the celebrations and headed up the procession to the house of God.

Third, the multitudes traveled with shouts of Joy and thanksgiving. The times of pilgrimage and worship were times of celebration in awareness that God had poured out many gifts upon his people. These times were uplifting as the people gratefully recalled together the character of their God.

Fourth, the poet says once again, "among the festive throng." The idea of the group both begins and ends his description of his memory. His emphasis upon that fact indicates that one of the best things about those times of worship was that he was among the others, celebrating together the magnificent love of God.

Quiet time alone is vitally important; however, it is also necessary at times *not* to be alone in worship. Our spirits crave corporate worship, a throng of people celebrating together.

The refrain of these psalms moves dramatically from despair and discouragement to the great *yet* of "Put your hope in God, for I will yet praise him, my Savior and my God." The poet seems to realize that one of the solutions for his being downcast and disturbed is to get together with the people of God. Praising God will usher in again a time of hope.

Surely that matches our experience. When we are deeply depressed over failure or rejection in our lives, times of worship with an assembly or small group and times of prayer with others are some of the greatest means for uplifting us. When the soul is thronged with doubts and despair, comfort is found in the fellowship of the throngs of the saints.

The poet tries to calm his soul by reminding himself that soon he will be able to worship. The verb root *to wait* is put in a form that extends it to mean "to hope." The word that we translate "yet" expresses addition or repetition, the fact of more. *Yet* the poet will be able to praise God, who is his personal Savior and God. He is indeed *my* God, the poet says (literally, "the deliverer of my face"), so he looks forward to praising him. The psalmist knows that such an action will help to ease his discouragement and free his disturbed spirit.

We are necessarily skipping over many other themes in Psalm 42, in order to focus specifically upon the theme of worship as it bridges the two psalms of the poem. You might want to observe carefully some of the other main themes, such as prayer, deliverance from enemies, and so forth, in your own daily devotions.

In Psalm 43 the third verse brings us back again to the theme of corporate worship. The poet asks God to send out his light and truth. The verb *to send* implies a commissioning, a being sent for a specific purpose, which is, in this case, to guide the poet.

Light is a common concept in the Psalms (and, of course, similarly in the teachings of Jesus). Figuratively, light is needed for guidance. When coupled with the idea of truth, which also implies faithfulness, the pair of words stresses that the poet needs to be able to discern what is best for his life. He begs God (the Hebrew is strong with "let them" and an emphatic pronoun) to allow his light and truth to lead him in the path of happiness. Particularly, he seeks the leading that will bring him for worship to the mountain of holiness.

The poet's asking for light and truth might imply that he longs for God's guidance in order to find a holy mountain wherever he might be. The psalmist wants intensely to be able to go to the place where God dwells so that he can meet with him. Specifically, he longs for the special feast times at the temple in Jerusalem, but the stanza can also be interpreted in a broader sense to mean any gatherings of the assembly for worship.

Furthermore, he asks particularly for the opportunity to go to the altar. Since only the priests were able to do so, we discover now that the poet was probably one of the officials for the worship services. This is especially implied when he asks to be able to praise God with his harp. Perhaps he was one of the temple musicians and longs for the day when he can play for the celebrations again. According to the title, these psalms come from the "Sons of Korah," who were a part of the descendants of Levi in charge of the music when David was king (see 1 Chron. 6).

That longing is part of my experience, too. Playing the organ for a festival service on Christmas Eve was my happy privilege last December for the first time in several years. There is in us a deep desire to use our gifts in the praise and worship of our God.

That is why we can see an important connection between our loneliness and our need for worship when the poet again speaks the refrain of his discouragement and then the word of hope. We join him in looking to worship for the praise way out of loneliness and despair.

Worship is not a panacea to cure forever our being downcast. It will not bring to an end our loneliness. But worship does offer us the way to meet a triple need—our longings for closer communion with God, for deeper fellowship with his people, and for the opportunity to use our gifts to express praise. This is why we can continue to hope in disturbing times: For surely we will yet praise him. We will know him as our personal Savior and God as we join together with other believers in the assembly of praise.

FOR FURTHER MEDITATION

1. What other themes do I see in these psalms that I might want to study on my own?
2. How have I experienced the longing about which the poet speaks?
3. How is corporate worship a healing agent for loneliness?
4. Why does the poet need God's light and truth to guide him to the holy mountain? Why can't he find it himself?
5. Why do I need God's light and truth to guide me?
6. In what ways would I like to deepen my participation in corporate worship?
7. How have I experienced the thrill of leading in worship—through singing or playing a musical instrument or reading or making a banner or any other means? How did that experience affect my spiritual and personal life?

26. Finding the Strength to Go On

Ascribe to the LORD, O mighty ones,
  ascribe to the LORD glory and strength.
Ascribe to the LORD the glory due his name;
  worship the LORD in the splendor of his holiness.
The voice of the LORD is over the waters;
  the God of glory thunders,
  the LORD thunders over the mighty waters.
The voice of the LORD is powerful;
  the voice of the LORD is majestic.
The voice of the LORD breaks the cedars. . . .
The voice of the LORD shakes the desert. . . .
And in his temple all cry, "Glory!"
The LORD sits enthroned over the flood;
  the LORD is enthroned as King forever.
The LORD gives strength to his people;
  the LORD blesses his people with peace.
                                  Psalm 29:1–5a, 8a, 9c–11

When the strength isn't there, it isn't there.

Probably the greatest frustration in my life is that when my blood pressure is too low and my metabolism too slow I just can't walk up—up hills, up stairs, up from a chair. I have enough strength; it just isn't available to me fast enough. That gets very discouraging, especially when the people around me don't understand and complain that I am too pokey. Too many bad experiences in past years of getting left behind resulted in a poor self-concept about it, so that I couldn't accept my own limitations, either. The lack of wholeness, therefore, was not so much in my body as in my spirit.

Psalm 29 offers immense comfort for all of us, no matter what kind of deficiency we might suffer. Perhaps you don't lack for strength, but you feel inferior to others in intelligence or in appearance or in social finesse. Whatever our weaknesses, they cause a lack of wholeness, and certainly the latter is the greater problem. Into the insecurity of all that, this psalm brings a tremendous word of hope.

Before considering its particular verses, however, we must this time look first at some forms of Hebrew poetry. Psalm 29 is one that is best read aloud to catch the impact of its parallel lines. Notice, for example, the parallelism of the first two verses. The phrase "ascribe to the LORD" occurs in the first three lines and is matched in the fourth by the phrase "worship the LORD." Then the second half of each of the lines contains a phrase about might and glory.

Next, the poetic structure revolves around seven uses of the phrase "the voice of the LORD," but notice in the psalm all the other poetic repetitions of key words. Finally, the last two verses use parallel expressions depicting the LORD sitting enthroned and announcing the gifts that the LORD gives to his people.

The final word, *shalom*, "peace," is accentuated by making it the final word—inverting the word order of the parallel line just above. By moving "his people" into the middle of the line and "peace" to the end, the poet gives more force than ever to that last word. All the impact of the literary buildup throughout the poem comes to a peak in that great word *shalom*.

Stop for a moment and read the whole psalm aloud from some version of the Bible that has set it up in poetic lines, and accentuate, as you read, all the poetic parallels. Notice the tremendous crescendo of power as the poem progresses. Altogether it creates a vivid picture of the immense strength of Yahweh as he handles all of creation and all of history with his majestic voice.

One of the greatest afflictions in our loneliness is the lack of strength, which often is the physical symptom of our emotional brokenness. "How can I find the strength to go on?" is a common question among those who suffer. Thus, we are powerfully encouraged by seeing all the elements in this psalm assuring us that the LORD will indeed provide us with all the strength that we need.

First of all, the angels are called to give God praise, for which he is eminently worthy. The phrase "O mighty ones" probably refers to the angels. The original text says, literally, "sons of the strong ones," and the root for the latter word is *el*, which means "god."

Why would the poet initially call upon the supernatural beings to worship the Lord properly? Perhaps he does that because the angels who are God's messengers know so much better all that his strength entails. They have been observing it and praising it for a long time, so, of course, they can do a much better job of praising than we can (especially since they do it from perfection, whereas we struggle with our humanity). The point for us, then, is to pay attention to them in order to learn more fully what the strength of Yahweh involves.

Next, we must note that the supernatural beings are called to ascribe to the Lord both glory and strength. The word *glory*, as we have seen in Chapter 20, means honor or reverence, putting Yahweh in his rightful position.

In the third line the word *glory* is expanded to remind us that it is due his name. Yahweh is supremely worthy of this ascription of praise because his character is glorious and mighty, as has been revealed not only to the angels, but also to us through history and in the Scriptures. Consequently, His character has become the object of our knowledge and love and praise.

The fourth poetic line stresses in its parallelism that the mighty beings are to bow down in worship, to prostrate themselves before Yahweh, "in the splendor of his holiness." This ambiguous phrase reminds us that an element of mystery infuses the majesty of worshiping an ineffable God.

The word *splendor* is always used in Old Testament texts in a construct form that is best translated, "adornment of." That Hebrew form links the word more tightly together with the following word for "holiness" or "apartness." The phrase together says, literally, "adornment of apartness," and stresses in connection with public worship that, when the praise of God is made known, the place where the praise is offered is made holy. We can understand this more clearly by looking at some similar uses of these words in 1 Chronicles 16:24, 2 Chronicles 20:21, and Psalm 96:9.

In all of these texts of adoration, notice in their contexts the

Joy and exuberance of the worship. To praise the LORD in the splendor of his holiness brings that deep sense of his apartness into the very place where we are worshiping and fills us with awe and wonder at his majesty.

Next, the mighty ones are reminded, as are we, of the magnificence of the voice of the LORD and what it has accomplished in the history of the world. The number seven in Jewish thought stands for completeness or perfection, so the seven pictures are vivid images of Yahweh in all the creative acts and historical deeds (represented symbolically) by which he has dealt powerfully with Israel. In the first use of the phrase *the voice of the LORD,* the repetition of the words *waters* and *thunders* sets up a graphic sound picture of God's creative word bringing the world into being from chaos. The word *glory,* moreover, links this section with the psalm's opening call to praise.

Next are images of storms and, probably, specifically the tremendous storm upon Sinai when Yahweh appeared there to make clear his covenant relationship with the people of Israel. His shaking of the desert of Kadesh reminds us that his children were brought out of the Egyptian bondage, kept by him through all their wanderings in that wilderness, and made a special people by his words to them at the great mountain.

No wonder all the angels respond, "Glory!" All the hosts of heaven have been reminded that he has used his voice in these powerful ways. Therefore, all the dwellers in his temple must shout out "the glory due his name."

We who are worshiping in our earthly temples respond, too, with "Glory!" Certainly we are impressed with the extent of the LORD's might when we observe the strength of merely his voice. All the things that he has accomplished by a simple word must enable us to realize the immensity of his total strength.

This final picture is added to the montage: The LORD sat enthroned over the flood. At the time of the Flood, God was completely in control; therefore, he could promise that such a flood would never take place again. He was, after all, in charge. The word for "flood" that appears in this tenth verse occurs nowhere else in the Scriptures except in the Genesis account of the story of Noah and the Flood. For that reason, we can be reasonably sure that the poet is referring to that particular flood when he says here that Yahweh was enthroned over it.

That is proof, David seems to say by the addition of the poetic parallel, that Yahweh also sits enthroned over all events. He sits enthroned as King of the universe and forever. Not only does he rule over all space and nature, but also he reigns over all time and history.

Now what are the consequences of this tremendous strength? We have seen by a colossal crescendo of magnificent images just how strong the great LORD and King of the universe is. Now, specifically, we are reminded personally that the LORD chooses graciously to give that strength to his people. This is another sentence that we must frequently hear to realize the impact of its meaning: Yahweh *does give* strength to his people.

The verb *gives* is in the imperfect tense in the Hebrew, which means that the action is incomplete. That could signify either that he will give it in the future or that he is constantly giving it. I very much prefer this NIV rendition with a present continuing verb: "The LORD gives strength to his people." We can count on it now. The simple answer to that terrible question, "How can I find the strength to go on?" is this strong assurance: "Yahweh gives strength to his people."

Finally, the culmination of this overwhelmingly encouraging psalm is the poetic parallel to the promise of strength. Not only does Yahweh give us the strength that we need, but, moreover, he blesses us with peace.

When I struggle against slow metabolism and low blood pressure, not only do I need the strength to keep going, but, more than that, I need the wholeness that will allow me to accept myself in my limitations. That is the promise of this final line of the poem—so mightily emphasized by the placement of the word *shalom* at the very end of the psalm. The greatest blessing of Yahweh to his people is the gift of *shalom*.

The noun *shalom* is one of the largest concepts in the Old Testament. We do the word an injustice if we limit it to the idea of "peace," although that is where it begins. First of all, *shalom* means reconciliation with God. Then, because of that peace, his people can have peace with their neighbors, in the sense of absence of war, and with themselves. Such peace issues further in both health and wealth—health because the body is spared from the psychosomatic effects of anxiety and discord, and wealth because the mind is free to enjoy the richness of blessings received.

These concepts, in turn, lead to definitions of tranquility, satisfaction, contentment, and fulfillment. A good summary of all these meanings is the word *wholeness,* which is what we long for most deeply as we search for healing and freedom from loneliness.

Finally, the word *shalom* contains within it the promise of commitment. If we say *shalom* to someone and mean it sincerely, we are committing ourselves to that person so that whatever we might have that he or she needs to be whole, we will gladly give it. James seems to allude to this concept of *shalom* when he writes as follows:

> What does it profit, my brethren, if a man says he has faith but has not works? Can his faith save him? If a brother or sister is ill-clad and in lack of daily food, and one of you says to them, "Go in peace, be warmed and filled," without giving them the things needed for the body, what does it profit?
>
> *James 2:14–16, Revised Standard Version*

Shalom includes making the commitment that is necessary to provide what is needed for such wholeness to be secured.

As we conclude our study of Psalm 29, we draw the mountain of images to a snowy peak in the largeness of the *shalom* with which God blesses his people. Yahweh creates for us reconciliation with himself and, consequently, the peace with our neighbors and with ourselves that leads to health, wealth, tranquility, contentment, fulfillment, and wholeness. He is committed to all of that in us, so that, when he gives us the strength to go on, he also gives us the healing to overcome whatever hinders our strength.

He gives us not only the physical power, but also the spiritual and emotional and psychological ability to continue. The fullness of his *shalom* frees us to accept our limitations and rest in his strength. After all, his voice can make the whole forest of

Lebanon dance. Certainly that strength will enable us to dance again, too.

FOR FURTHER MEDITATION

1. What is the value of such a poetic crescendo in this psalm?
2. Why should the angels be called upon to sing Yahweh's praise?
3. Why is glory due his name?
4. What does it mean to worship the LORD in the splendor of his holiness?
5. What specific instances in Old Testament history are called to mind by the "voice of the LORD" passages?
6. How does the fact that Yahweh was enthroned over the flood enable me to trust his enthronement over all situations in my life?
7. How does the fact that Yahweh adds *shalom* to the strength that he gives us make it larger for me? Why is the gift of *shalom* such a strengthening gift?

27. Comfort Even When There Is No Assurance

But when I was silent and still,
   not even saying anything good,
   my anguish increased.
My heart grew hot within me,
   and as I meditated, the fire burned;
   then I spoke with my tongue:
"Show me, O LORD, my life's end
   and the number of my days;
   let me know how fleeting is my life.
You have made my days a mere handbreadth;
   the span of my years is as nothing before you.
   Each man's life is but a breath.   *Selah*
Man is a mere phantom as he goes to and fro;
   He bustles about, but only in vain;
   he heaps up wealth, not knowing who will get it.
But now, Lord, what do I look for?
   My hope is in you.
Save me from all my transgressions. . . .
Remove your scourge from me;
   I am overcome by the blow of your hand.
You rebuke and discipline men for their sin;
   you consume their wealth like a moth—
   each man is but a breath.   *Selah*
Hear my prayer, O LORD,
   listen to my cry for help;
   be not deaf to my weeping.
For I dwell with you as an alien,
   a stranger, as all my fathers were.
Look away from me, that I may rejoice again
   before I depart and am no more."
                              Psalm 39:2–8a, 10–13

We were hiking in the woods. My two older brothers had run on ahead to jump out and scare my parents and me when we caught up. But we had gone to the end of the trail and had not met them, in spite of all our calling. Were my brothers lost forever?

"No," my dad assured me calmly. "They will be all right." Nothing in the circumstances could convince me of that. But my father had said that my brothers would be safe, so I believed it with all of the energy of my five years. He had never been wrong before in my experience, so somehow in my fright I believed that he could make everything right.

Part of our loneliness can come from seeing absolutely no basis for assurance. But the poet here in Psalm 39 continues to hope, even though everything seems to be against him. Perhaps only Psalm 88 is darker. Describing the blackest of blacknesses, that psalm ends as follows:

> From my youth I have been afflicted and close to death;
>   I have suffered your terrors and am in despair.
> Your wrath has swept over me;
>   your terrors have destroyed me.
> All day long they surround me like a flood;
>   they have completely engulfed me.
> You have taken my companions and loved ones from me;
>   the darkness is my closest friend.
>
> *Psalm 88:15–18*

Why should we consider such gloomy psalms in a book that is intended to give comfort and hope and encouragement to those who are struggling against the despair of loneliness and depression and grief?

These psalms of despair are encouraging, first of all, because they help us to know that we are not alone. Other believers have struggled against seemingly insurmountable odds and yet were able to continue to believe.

However, that would not be sufficient comfort without another fact and another gloomy psalm. Psalm 22 begins with these words:

> My God, my God, why have you forsaken me?
>   Why are you so far from saving me,
>   so far from the words of my groaning?
> O my God, I cry out by day, but you do not answer,
>   by night, and am not silent.
> Yet. . . .
>
> *Psalm 22:1–3a*

Because this psalm was cried out by the One who changed our lives and destinies for us, we can find comfort in the despairing psalms. Though God seems to have forsaken us or we have no basis for assurance, yet we can trust, knowing the character of the One who speaks to us and what he has done to deliver us from this earth's sufferings.

Just this morning I was profoundly comforted in my devotional time by the assigned reading from the book of Hebrews. Let these words sink deeply into your sorrowing heart or troubled mind:

> Therefore, since we have a great high priest who has gone through the heavens, Jesus the Son of God, let us hold firmly to the faith we profess. For we do not have a high priest who is unable to sympathize with our weaknesses, but we have one who has been tempted in every way, just as we are—yet without sin. Let us then approach the throne of grace with confidence, so that we may receive mercy and find grace to help us in our time of need.
>
> *Heb. 4:14–16*

Sometimes we wake up sad. When we try to get past the grief and understand ourselves, we are overwhelmed by our list of sadnesses. Nothing gets sorted, and having no one with whom to share the pain makes us feel more lonely. What can the Psalms say to us in the midst of such anguish?

Jesus, in his pain, called out to the God who had forsaken him. And because he bore that total forsakenness for us, we know that we will never have to experience it. Like the poet in Psalm 39, we may speak out of despair, but we never have to speak out of abandonment. He recognizes God's chastising, but he also realizes that his sin has caused his state of woe.

You might be saying, "But I haven't sinned. I am the victim"—who has been rejected or deserted or treated cruelly or been underprivileged throughout life. Yet in the recognition that we are sinners and that God is God we can finally come to peace.

Stay with me while we hammer out this tough theology. I constantly wrestle with it because I want always to understand before I can accept circumstances in my life. Why does God let us go through such horrible pain?

Often when piles of things are making me sad, most of the

items on the list are things I don't understand. Why can't my housemate Julie find a job—doesn't God realize how discouraged she is getting? Why is singing for this wedding bringing back so many sad memories? Why can't I get past all this grief stuff?

Into the midst of such wrestling my friend Linden inserts this perspective: "I just believe that God is still in control and that he will bring good out of all things." Toward that simple fact of faith I grope. I long for the maturity—or simplicity—of faith that Linden possesses.

Linden's trust that God is in control is all the more profound because he is a quadriplegic, paralyzed by an automobile accident. A few years younger than I, he puts me to shame by the strength of his confidence in God—no matter what happens.

Many phrases in Psalm 39 show evidence of a similar faith, even in the midst of the poet's sadness. The fact of sin, the obstruction of human understanding, and the sureness of God's presence even in the greatest darkness are truths reinforced by this psalm's progression of thought.

Just after talking about the anguish and the burning that continued even when he was silent, in verse 4 the poet David addresses his God as LORD. Still he is the Covenant God. Specifically, he asks the LORD to show him his end and the measurement of his days. This is the only place in the Old Testament where the idea of measurement is used in terms of time. The psalmist is asking God to put him in touch with how ephemeral life is.

When he looks at the brevity of his life, he requests further instruction. He says, literally, to Yahweh, "Let me know how lacking I (am)." The idea of "lacking" comes from a root meaning "to cease"; it is rarely used as an adjective in the Old Testament, as it is here. Such a unique word stresses how much we need Yahweh to show us the inability of our transient existence to perpetuate itself and, consequently, our utter dependence upon him. When we come to such a point of absolute weakness and dependence, then we will get our priorities straight and be able to look up to the LORD for the gifts that he is able to bring out of even our deepest griefs.

This concept is accentuated in the Hebrew by the emphatic

pronoun *I* at the end of the sentence. *We* are the ones who are lacking.

Immediately, our human nature gets defensive. We object, "But I've been driven low enough. Why does God continue to allow me to be scourged?" Sometimes we sink to the depths of darkest despair recorded in Psalm 88.

Surely we dare not be superficial about the intense pain and violent anguish through which we pass. From experience, I know that the words "Well, we must get the right perspective" aren't very comforting. Nevertheless, because we fight so hard against being reduced to the point of total weakness, we don't really believe God for the good purposes he can bring out of the terrible things in our lives.

I learned that a few weeks ago when I taught a class on coping with divorce at a singles conference in Minneapolis. My best qualification for teaching that class is that I haven't coped very well. We considered the various dimensions of our existence— physical, emotional, psychological, social, intellectual, spiritual—and out of our brokenness began to minister to each other. God used the most horrible months of our lives to equip us to be sensitive to the pain of others.

Though I hated the months of dark despair that kept me so deeply depressed for so long (and still those moments strike me occasionally), yet now I realize that God was using even those times to draw me closer to himself, to teach me invaluable lessons about his love that I never could have learned otherwise, to create in me new sensitivity and care for the many people in the world who are hurting in terrible ways, to increase in me the desire to do something about that pain, and to give me new purpose in my existence and new goals for my life once my old basis of understanding had been destroyed.

Not everything feels good yet. But as I learn to believe God for what he is able to do with even the darkest times, I will become more able, in turn, to help others through their times of blackness.

Nevertheless, we first need the humbling, the recognition of the ephemerality of our lives so that they can be placed back into God's hands for his purposes. This is the poet's emphasis: "You have made my days a mere handbreadth, the span of my

years is as nothing before you. Each man's life is but a breath."
He is not saying that we aren't worth much. We are incredibly
valuable to the God who made us, but we are, after all, mere
human beings and not God. When we get that straight, we are
more able to trust him in the darkness.

That is why the poet continues, "Man is a mere phantom as
he goes to and fro; He bustles about, but only in vain; he heaps
up wealth, not knowing who will get it." The point is that our
frantic human efforts to find worth and meaning are empty.
The process itself is changed when we begin with the right
perspective and priorities. Therefore, the poet next makes this
plea: "But now, Lord, what do I look for? My hope is in you.
Save me from all my transgressions."

The phrase "surely in vain" or "surely a vapour" has re-
curred in this psalm three times—in verses 5, 6, and 11. Because of that, verse 7 states the alternative simply with the Hebrew introduction, "and now." This phrase means, "therefore,
drawing a conclusion from what has just been stated." In other
words, "since I have a proper awareness of my transience,
therefore, what am I looking for?"

It is significant that at this point the poet does not call God
by his covenant name. Instead, he uses the word *adonai*, which
means "Lord" in the sense of a master or ruler. Even outside of
the covenant relationship he recognizes that, after all, God is
the Lord. There is no one else to whom we can look. "My
hope," he declares, "to you it." The word *hope* here is derived
from the verb *to wait.* (That is the root used in the refrain in
verses 5 and 11 of Psalm 42 and verse 5 of Psalm 43. See Chapter 25.) No one else is worth waiting for. Nothing else can give
us a hope that does not disappoint (see Rom. 5:5). Nothing else
deserves our eager searching.

From our sin we must be freed. Therefore, the poet continues, "Save me from all my transgressions." "Transgressions"
comes from the verb *to rebel.* The poet recognizes that our rebellious nature refuses to wait for God to bring good out of our
hurts and struggles. We want to work things out by our own
methods, and we thereby block the LORD's guidance and trans-
forming love.

Consequently, the poet concludes with a plea for the LORD

(using the name of the covenant God again) to hear his prayer, to listen to his cry for help, to be not deaf to his weeping. Though he feels like an alien and a stranger, yet he knows that he dwells with Yahweh.

My Hebrew dictionary defines the phrase "with you" from this passage in terms of being "in the service of" or "of the house or family of." Notice that this meaning implies a close connection, even though David feels like an alien. This is a key for us in our blackest times: Though we feel like strangers with God, yet he has deigned to make us part of his family. Still he is our covenant God. When we can put our sin and his grace into proper perspective, we have made a giant step toward healing.

We can't expect to be out of depression immediately or think that there should be no more sadness. Wounds are deep, and despair can be profound. Yet our hope is in the LORD, even though—with the poet—we wish he would look away from us for a moment to give us relief from the truth.

FOR FURTHER MEDITATION

1. How have I understood the problem of pain?
2. What is the value of knowing the transience of my life?
3. How can it be helpful in despair to acknowledge my sin?
4. In what other things do I sometimes place my hope?
5. How do I try to solve my own problems? What is the result of my own devices?
6. How can I turn to the LORD when it feels like I am an alien or sojourner with him?
7. How do I know that the LORD will hear my prayer and not be deaf to my weeping?

28. Putting Our Grief into Historical Perspective

I thought about the former days,
  the years of long ago;
I remembered my songs in the night.
  My heart mused and my spirit inquired:
"Will the Lord reject us forever?
  Will he never show his favor again?
Has his unfailing love vanished forever?
  Has his promise failed for all time?
Has God forgotten to be merciful?
  Has he in anger withheld his compassion?"   *Selah*
Then I thought, "To this I will appeal:
  the years of the right hand of the Most High."
I will remember the deeds of the LORD;
  yes, I will remember your miracles of long ago.
I will meditate on all your works
  and consider all your mighty deeds.
Your ways, O God, are holy.
  What god is so great as our God?
You are the God who performs miracles;
  you display your power among the peoples.
With your mighty arm you redeemed your people,
  the descendants of Jacob and Joseph.   *Selah*
                              Psalm 77:5–15

"I just can't take it any more," I whimpered.

My friend Marguerite gently chided, "I wish I had a tape recording of all the times you have said that and then gone on." She then proceeded to remind me of many of the times in the long trek toward healing when I had become so discouraged that I felt I couldn't handle life any more. "But each time God gave you the strength to keep going."

Marguerite is one of the friends who has helped me most to bear the pain of divorce. We met at the church where I worked before I became a free-lance teacher. We became good friends because of common interests in Bible study and classical music, but I grew to love her deeply in gratitude for her insightful mind and gentle support. When things began to fall apart in my personal life, she noticed that something was wrong and invited me to talk. Sitting in a rocking chair in her family room, I poured out all the grief that had been bottled up in my heart for so long. Soon her rocking chair became a frequent haven for me, and often as I sat there I cried that I could not go on. Each time her comforting words and presence sustained me and gave me courage.

We must learn to put our grief and loneliness into a historical perspective. In remembering ways that God has helped us in the past we can find comfort for the present and hope for the future.

That is what the poet does in Psalm 77. As the poet grieves from some unknown distress, he pauses to put his trouble into historical perspective so that he can trust God to rescue him from the trial he is undergoing now.

The poet deals with his grief and troubled spirit with a firm discipline of mind. The verb *to think* is used in the first verse of this section in an intensified form that means more deeply to consider or to be mindful of something. The poet's mind was focused on the past, the previous ages in which God's love had been clearly seen. God's dramatic deeds on behalf of his people were the subject of many songs of faith, to which the poet might be referring when he says that he remembered his songs in the night.

His self-discipline is further reflected in the fourth line: "My heart mused and my spirit inquired." "The heart" is used here to mean the inner person, the comprehending mind and will. Though we use it in English simply to signify emotions, the word *heart* in Hebrew emphasizes thinking and reflection, the objective basis for our subjective affections. Thus, to muse with one's heart means to meditate upon or to study.

The word translated "inquired" in the NIV is an intensification of the Hebrew word *to search*. The noun *spirit* is used in some of the later poems of the Old Testament to denote the organ for mental acts, but in the context of this psalm there are also connotations of a troubled disposition. When the poet struggles against his doubts and fears and wonderings, he responds to that troubling in his spirit with disciplined searching for the truth.

This offers us a wonderful model, very much in keeping with all that we have been learning in these meditations upon the Psalms. We dare not let ourselves be so overwhelmed by our emotions that our reason is incapacitated. The best way to deal with ourselves in our grief is to be able to put things into proper perspective and, thereby, to find comfort and hope.

Next, the poet asks six profound rhetorical questions. Each one is so worded that we want to shout phrases of utter disbelief: "*No!* Of course not! Who could imagine such a thing? We know better." Carefully listen to these questions in a more literal translation that more clearly emphasizes their point:

> To everlastingnesses will the Lord reject us?
> Will he not do it again to be pleased with us any more?
> Has his *chesedh* [loving-kindness and steadfast faithfulness]
>   ceased to perpetuity?
> Has the word come to an end for age upon age?
> Has he forgotten to show favor [or bestow his loving
>   redemption]—God?
> Or has he shut up [closed in] in anger his compassions? *Selah*

The word *Selah* at the end of the strophe causes us to pause, too, and consider these questions. They stir us almost to an angry response. Our God isn't like that. Could God forget to show favor—God? That would be a contradiction in terms. No! he hasn't forgotten. No! this can't last forever. No! he hasn't closed in his compassions toward us.

The poet discloses how ridiculously obvious the answers to those questions are when he continues with an appeal to many "years of the right hand of the Most High." This name is often used for God in the Psalms, and the entire phrase refers to all the time the poet has spent in the place of intimacy with this highest and only God.

We worry about loneliness or grief in terms of days or months; in contrast, we need to learn the habit of remembering the LORD's love in terms of years. Think for a while of your own history. How has God led your family through crisis and through difficult circumstances in order to preserve them? How have you personally seen his faithful love over the long haul?

For example, I think of how my grandmother escaped with her family from Russia, wandered all over Europe, went to Argentina, and finally wound up in Canada, where she married her eighth-grade teacher. Consequently, my father and many relatives have all been dedicated Lutheran schoolteachers, so that the love of the Scriptures has been in my bones since childhood. God led me from teaching Literature of the Bible at a university, through the back door into campus ministry, and then into a parish, and finally into free-lancing.

What gratitude is stirred when we look back over the years of the right hand of the Most High! Even if your family are not people of faith, I am sure that you can see God's protecting and guiding hand in some of the events that have brought you to your present position in life.

In the next four lines, the poet uses four different Hebrew words (in English, "deeds," "miracles," "works," and "mighty deeds") to name the works of the LORD. Notice that only in the first line of these four is the name *Yahweh* used in this psalm. Significantly, here the psalmist recounts deeds as the works of a Covenant God, who is faithful in his relationship with his people.

The first and the last words for his works ("deeds" and "mighty deeds") are unusual because they both come from a Hebrew root that is usually associated with bad practices. The word for "mighty deeds" actually means "wantonnesses." Just as a prostitute is too generous with herself, so God's goodness is so outrageously profligate that he seems sinfully wanton with it. We saw this word in Chapter 23 used negatively, to describe the evil deeds in which we don't want to become involved.

This powerful image means that God is prodigal with his benefits. But when we think about our own histories that seems to be a good description. God is absolutely crazy in how much he loves us. Some people might be offended at the use of such words to describe the holy God, but truly it makes no sense that he could love us with such outrageous generosity.

The second word, translated "miracles," literally means "extraordinaries" and denotes things hard to understand because they fill us with so much awe (see Chapter 22).

Only the third word is an ordinary one. It simply means "works" or "doings." In that very simplicity, however, it reminds us that God does everything—even the simple little things that we would think were too low for him. Thus, the poet says, "I will meditate on all your works."

"Remember," in this set of four lines about Yahweh's works, can also mean "to cause to be remembered," "to praise them publicly," "to mention them to others to commemorate them." "Meditate" and "consider" underscore the value of private musing upon the prodigality of God's works.

Notice all the thinking that is involved. The New Testament similarly emphasizes the renewal of our minds (see, for example, Rom. 12:1–2). The poet urges us to be more objective about our troubles so that we can put them into a godly and comforting perspective.

The poet summarizes all his discoveries about the actions of God in "Your ways, O God, are holy." Our own perspectives sometimes are not. The Hebrew text is a bit more dramatic. It says, literally, "O God, in holiness your way." His moral administration of the universe is founded in sacredness or apartness. Consequently, we can all recognize that there is no other god so great as he. When the poet asks, "What god is so great as our God?" this last rhetorical question with the earlier ones brings the sum of seven to completion. All seven of the questions are answered by all the evidence of ancient, past, modern, and future history.

After all, God is the one who is doing the wonders, the poet continues. He makes his strength known among all the people by taking care of his own children, the descendants of Jacob and Joseph. As we pause at the "Selah" after this strophe, we consider why in this place Israel is referred to as the descendants of Jacob and Joseph. *Jacob* records their lineage and reminds the people of Yahweh's covenant relationship with Abraham, Isaac, and Jacob. *Joseph* is a reminder of God's loving provision for the Israelites in Egypt as he used Jacob's son to save the world through his wise storing of grain for the time of famine.

This entitling of the people is a fitting prelude to the next several verses, which recount other deeds as God led his people out of the Egyptian captivity. The poet goes on to describe in vivid terms the crossing of the Red Sea, the covenant promises of Sinai, the crossing of the Jordan, the leadership of Moses and Aaron. Certainly, if God so led his people through all those events of the Exodus, he can lead them now—perhaps out of the Babylonian captivity, if that is when the poet writes.

Because we do not know the specific historical setting of this poem, we can perhaps more easily transfer its words into our own particular circumstances. Pausing to remember how God took care of his people in the past, we gather together a historical perspective that enables us to cope with our own griefs and troubles in these times.

When the Children of Israel crossed the Jordan River successfully to enter into the Promised Land, the LORD told them to gather stones for each tribe and to build an altar as a memorial. Joshua told them to do this "to serve as a sign among you. In the future when your children ask you, 'What do these stones mean?' tell them that the flow of the Jordan was cut off before the ark of the covenant of the LORD . . . . These stones are to be a memorial to the people of Israel forever" (Josh. 4:6–7).

Because of this and other Old Testament stories, we are encouraged to create memorials. I write a poem or learn a song or buy a book I've always wanted to buy and inscribe it with significant events in my spiritual life, physical circumstances, or emotional healing; whenever I look at that memorial I can remember the LORD's deeds of long ago and be encouraged for today. Whenever we review the past, we have to come to this conclusion: "Your ways, O God, are holy." Grief put into historical perspective is bearable. When we ask, "How can I go on?" the answer is the same as the last time: "The LORD will give you the strength." We know that he will; we have seen it happen time and again.

FOR FURTHER MEDITATION

1. Of what events in my life might I build a memorial to remember God's deeds? How have I seen God's action in the history of my family or nation or people?
2. What is the importance of my mind in coping with grief or trouble?
3. How would I answer the seven questions the poet asks?
4. In what ways are God's acts profligate? How do I feel about using the term *wanton* to describe his deeds?
5. What does it mean to call God's ways holy? How are they set apart?
6. What stories about Israel appeal to me as good examples of God's dealing with his people in their history?
7. What habits of meditation would I like to develop so that my perspective about my life can be more objective?

29. The LORD Will Give Us the Desires of Our Hearts

Trust in the LORD and do good;
  dwell in the land and enjoy safe pasture.
Delight yourself in the LORD
  and he will give you the desires of your heart.
Commit your way to the LORD;
  trust in him and he will do this:
He will make your righteousness shine like the dawn,
  the justice of your cause like the noonday sun.

Psalm 37:3–6

One kind of loneliness strikes when we feel as though we're the only ones trying to secure justice in a messed-up world. How can our cause be vindicated? When we get discouraged, everything and everyone around seems corrupt.

Psalm 37 is a wisdom poem that announces vindication, written in the form of an acrostic, in which every verse begins with the next letter of the Hebrew alphabet. We must see the few verses that we are considering here in light of the context of the whole psalm.

Throughout Psalm 37 the phrase "do not fret" occurs frequently. In the introductory verses, the wise poet reminds us that we don't have to fret, first of all, because the evil ones, like the grass, will soon wither away. (See our study of Psalm 73 in Chapter 18 for related ideas concerning our reactions to those who choose wrong.) As Isaiah says, "All flesh is grass."*

After that encouraging reminder to avoid worrying, the poet now turns to the positive side in the verses before us and tells what to do instead. His plan for action might not change our condition of being alone, but it can turn our painful loneliness into beneficial solitude.

---

*See my comments on this verse from Isaiah 40 in chapters 6–8 of my book *To Walk and Not Faint* (Chappaqua, N.Y.: Christian Herald Books, 1980).

First of all, he urges us to trust in the LORD, a phrase that we have seen often before (in chapter 1, for example), and then he exhorts us to do good. The significant order here reminds us that we don't do good out of our ability to do good, but out of our trusting. Our relationship with Yahweh enables us to produce what is morally good and of benefit to others. Though the verb *to do* basically means to accomplish or perform, it sometimes carries added connotations of creating. The phrase "do good," then, implies an invitation to cooperate with the Creator in accomplishing his purposes in the world.

The second poetic line invites us to inhabit the land and enjoy safe pasture. I prefer the New American Standard Version for this sentence because it stresses that when we "dwell in the land," we can "cultivate faithfulness" or, as the NASV adds in the footnotes, "feed on security or feed on His faithfulness." The Hebrew text says, "feed upon faithfulness," in the sense of consuming, or taking pleasure in, or nourishing oneself by steadfastness or fidelity.

The NIV rendering, "safe pasture," gives us a picture of this concept. When the Israelites inhabited the Promised Land, they were encouraged to live also within the principles of the covenant with Yahweh that would enable them to be secure in that land. Their pastures would be safe if they continued being the People of God.

Another implication of the text is that those who dwell in the land are able to observe in the seasons of rain and sunshine and in the harvest the faithfulness of Yahweh. Thus, the safety of the pasture is more deeply *enjoyed* by those who recognize the LORD who makes it secure.

For those of us who read this psalm in the twentieth century, these words continue to convey a sense of security. Though few of us live in the countryside, where we know the value of safe pastures, we do long for the stability that the image offers. We can rely on the fidelity of our God. As long as we are trusting in him, we will be empowered to do good, to dwell wherever he has called us, and to enjoy being nourished by his steadfastness.

This ties in very closely with the psalm's next point: That kind of security in the faithfulness of the LORD is much more available to those who supremely delight in him. We must intensify the English translation, "delight yourself in the LORD," because it means "to take exquisite delight" in him. The Hebrew word is an intensive reflexive (Hithpael) form of a verb that means "to be of dainty habit." It does not mean that believers are effeminate or wishy-washy. Rather, it means that their delight is so sensitive that it catches the softest nuances of God's love.

That idea challenges us, as Christians, to grow so close to the LORD that we would be delicately aware of his presence and guidance and gifting in even the tiniest circumstances of our lives. This would be to delight in him thoroughly.

Once when I was explaining this concept at a church in Seattle, a participant in the seminar told me of a time during his visit to New Zealand when a very delicate tea was served. Most of the American tourists loaded it with sugar and cream and then complained that it had no flavor. Similarly, he said, many Christians load up their lives with the sugars and creams of luxury and then are unable to see the delicate ways in which God is working in their lives.

We who live in a wealthy country have so many things and so many varieties of things that we have lost our appreciation for them. We clutter our houses with too many possessions rather than thoroughly enjoying a few. The unsatisfied longing in our lives keeps us thinking we need more; consequently, we don't appreciate the finer points of what we have. Even in our accomplishments, we start thinking about greater goals and become dissatisfied.

In our spiritual lives, we frequently do not delight so thoroughly in the LORD that he is the whole focus of our existence. Consequently, we find it difficult to enjoy the present delicacies of his relationship with us.

Notice that when we do delight ourselves in him he will give us the desires of our hearts. That is because our desires will be his. The closer we are to him, the more we will want only what he wants.

We might have to wrestle with this truth, especially when we're lonely. We may believe we want our desires to be Yahweh's desires, but still we might think, "Why does it have to be this way, LORD? Why can't you give me someone to ease my loneliness?" Perhaps we can't yet understand his best purposes for us. If we were thoroughly delighted with him in the first place, our needs wouldn't grow so horrendously out of proportion.

We dare not be glib, however, or give merely superficial comfort to ease the pain of lonely longings. The fact that God will give us the desires of our hearts is a truth we might know in our heads, but often don't feel. Nevertheless, to proclaim this truth can encourage us to keep going on in the struggle to believe it. We will come to the point someday of resting in that truth and finding our longings stilled with the deepest *shalom*.

The psalm's next phrase, which the NIV translates "Commit your way to the LORD," is originally a very graphic image. The Hebrew text actually says, "Roll unto Yahweh your way." To roll it as one rolls stones into a groove puts our way firmly into place. Then we can't grab it back and continue to fret about it. If we can thoroughly roll our conduct or mode of life or concerns upon Yahweh and trust in him, the poet continues, then he will act. As long as we are hanging on to things, we are preventing him from accomplishing his purposes. How much are we holding God up by our stubborn insistence that we know better how to do things?

Most translations conclude verse 5 with a colon, so that the phrase "He will do this" leads directly into the fact that he will make our righteousness shine like the dawn. That connection is true; one of the things that he will do is make our righteousness shine. However, I think that we limit the psalm too much if we tie those two concepts together insistently. Especially because the verb *to do* is the same one that appeared in the phrase "do good" in verse 3, we must simply say that if we roll our way unto the LORD, then he will act. Not only will he make our righteousness to shine like the dawn—although definitely that—but also he will accomplish much more. He will take care of everything that is associated with our "way." When we trust him, we can do good because he is the one doing it through us.

The New American Standard Version does not tie the two verses so closely together, but simply states that when we trust in the LORD "He will do it." The word *it* could mean anything, and that is a good ambiguity. God will do whatever our desires require because when we thoroughly commit everything to him and are exquisitely delighting in him, then what we desire will be his good purposes entirely.

Specifically, one of his good purposes will be to make our righteousness shine like the dawn. When we care for the needy, protest military aggression, or fight injustices in our society, our causes will be vindicated. Look at Mother Teresa, or the World Vision hospital in Cambodia, or the mission of MAP International to provide equipment and medicines in destitute countries, or the work of Chuck Colson's Prison Fellowship. Righteousness does, indeed, shine like the dawn.

Moreover, as the parallel poetic line promises, the justice of our cause will be like the noonday sun. The Hebrew is actually plural, which suggests that the sunshine is intensified so much that its glow seems like "noons." The Jerusalem Bible says, "making your virtue clear as the light, your integrity as bright as noon." The words *virtue* and *integrity* stress the goodness and wholeness of righteousness and justice. The Living Bible also presents a vivid picture in these words: "Your innocence will be clear to everyone. He will vindicate you with the blazing light of justice shining down as from the noonday sun."

Notice, finally, that again it is the LORD who accomplishes this, for indeed it is he (emphatic pronoun in the Hebrew) who is doing the acting. He will exhibit to the world as a light our righteousness. The verb *make* in this verse actually means that he publishes the justice of our cause.

The emphasis in all of this is an invitation to us to keep on keeping on—doing good, being righteous and just, committing our way to Yahweh, and trusting that the publishing, the vindicating, the results of all our efforts are up to him. All we need to be concerned about is that we are thoroughly delighting in the LORD so that the deepest desires of our being are tied in with his faithfulness.

FOR FURTHER MEDITATION

1. Why is the order of "Trust in the LORD and do good" so important?
2. How do I nourish myself with faithfulness?

3. What is it like to take exquisite delight in Yahweh?
4. What are the deepest desires of my heart?
5. What matters have I "rolled" unto Yahweh? What matters have I taken back?
6. How has my righteousness been made by him to shine like the dawn?
7. What do I do if my justice is not vindicated? Has Yahweh failed me then?

30. When I Fret and Fall, There Is *Shalom*

Be still before the LORD and wait patiently for him;
   do not fret when men succeed in their ways,
   when they carry out their wicked schemes. . . .
The LORD delights in the way of the man
   whose steps he has made firm;
though he stumble, he will not fall,
   for the LORD upholds him with his hand. . . .
Consider the blameless, observe the upright;
   there is a future for the man of peace.
                              Psalm 37:7, 23–24, 37

Rest in the LORD and wait patiently for Him;
   Fret not yourself because of him who prospers in his way,
   Because of the man who carries out wicked schemes. . . .
The steps of a man are established by the LORD;
   And He delights in his way.
When he falls, he shall not be hurled headlong;
   Because the LORD is the One who holds his hand. . . .
Mark the blameless man, and behold the upright;
   For the man of peace will have a posterity.
                              Psalm 37:7, 23–24, 37,
                              New American Standard Version

Usually in our agitations we are not very quiet. When we cannot be restful, we are not very able to wait patiently before the LORD. The result is that we miss many of his gifts because we are too frantic to hear his voice.

I like to call my devotional practices quiet time, to remind me that this block of time is set apart in order to let God speak, so that my ways are not my own devising. All these verses from scattered parts of Psalm 37 deal with the need for those who are struggling against the wickedness of evil to learn to rest in the LORD. These verses can be especially helpful in coping with loneliness because they bring us the intimate presence of a LORD who cares enough to sustain us in these tough times. His presence transforms our being alone into a solitude that actively listens rather than a loneliness that passively feels pain.

The first phrase literally says to "be silent to Yahweh," in the sense of the opposite of activity and motion or speech. Sometimes this happens naturally, as when a person is astounded in amazement or fear and therefore is silent before the LORD. The idea is like that of resignation, but without any of its negative connotations. Perhaps "Acceptance-with-Joy" (to borrow a phrase from Hannah Hurnard's *Hind's Feet on High Places*) is a better designation.

The verb that the NIV translates "wait patiently" comes from a Hebrew root that means "to dance or whirl" and is used at times to depict severe pain, as at childbirth. In the form used here it means "to suffer or writhe in torture" or "to wait with profound longing." Patience is implied in this waiting, but it is also filled with the tension of longing for release, even as a mother writhes through labor as she waits for the birth of her child.

That concept has much significance in our spiritual lives. We live in the between times—days and years between the moment or progression when Christ became the center and focus of our existence and the time when he will come again or we will die and go home to be with him. So how do we live in the meantime? Christ didn't call us to any easy Christianity, a comfortable "I'm saved" lifestyle that isn't intensely wrapped up in the work of his kingdom. Rather, as we wait for our LORD to come back, we wait with eager longing and anguish, for often what surrounds us is corrupted. Our own loneliness accentuates the brokenness of the world around us. When it is transformed instead into solitude that listens to Yahweh, we acquire the courage and power to wait for his final answers.

Next, the poet encourages us to lay aside our fretting "when men succeed in their ways." The original verb root for "fret" means "to be kindled" and is often used in connection with anger. Thus, it encourages us not to burn ourselves out in vexation. But once again, we must do some careful distinguishing. We *should* be angry—and not just mildly—against injustices, such as world hunger, for example.

Nevertheless, our frustration with the wickedness around us

must serve only for kindling purposes, to encourage our active involvement in fighting evil, not to start a huge fire of vexation that burns out of control and immobilizes us. Our efforts to combat evil are thwarted if we forget that ultimately God is in control of the world.

We are not to fret, the poet says, "when men succeed in their ways, when they carry out their wicked schemes." That wickedness seems to triumph is a reality, and a very painful one. However, those who love the LORD know a greater reality, in which we find our composure and are guided to channel our energies constructively. If it seems that the wicked are prospering in their ways, it is all the more imperative that we not be immobilized by it. Rather, as we learn to let Yahweh establish our steps, they will be effective in combating the injustice.

The word order in the New American Standard Version for verse 23 matches more closely the original Hebrew text, which begins with "from Yahweh the steps of a man are established": Yahweh's name comes first. When we make our relationship with him our top priority, then our course of life is established so that we are living out our principles more faithfully. The verb about being established is from a root that means "to be firm." In its form here and in the perfect tense (which implies completed action), the word stresses preparation and fixing. If we can learn to be silent before Yahweh, he will not be thwarted in his purpose to guide us and firmly root our ways.

Once, when I was on a ferry, a moment of silence allowed an organizing principle to surface in my thinking, and everything I'd been mulling over clicked into place. By the time we reached the dock, my teaching outline was prepared. Experiences like this help us see that only in stillness can we receive what the LORD has prepared.

Next, this psalm promises that the LORD delights in our way. Moreover, says the poet, not only do we know the encouragement of his delight in us, but also we can be sure that we will never be destroyed while seeking to be obedient to his purposes: literally, "Though he fall, not will he be hurled headlong."

A person might fall from weakness or battle wounds, but he or she will not be hurled like a javelin. Such protection from extreme violence reminds us of this hopeful sequence from Paul's second letter to the Corinthians:

> We are hard pressed on every side, but not crushed; perplexed, but not in despair; persecuted, but not abandoned; struck down, but not destroyed.
>
>   *2 Cor. 4:8–9*

J. B. Phillips paraphrases the passage in this way:

> We are handicapped on all sides, but we are never frustrated; we are puzzled, but never in despair. We are persecuted, but we never have to stand it alone; we may be knocked down but we are never knocked out.

The next line of the psalm tells us *why* we can know for sure that we will not be destroyed, though we might have to suffer. Yahweh upholds with his hand the one whose steps he is establishing. The verb *upholds* actually means "to lean or rest or support"; its participial form stresses the continuing nature of Yahweh's sustaining action.

Since the Hebrew word *his-hand* has no preposition with it, we cannot be certain whether the word is referring to Yahweh's hand or to the believer's. The NIV assumes the former and states that "the Lord upholds him with his hand." The New American Standard Version, on the other hand (pun intended), assumes the latter and translates, "the Lord is the one who holds his hand."

With either interpretation the comfort is tender. Yahweh supports us with his personal attention. The tangible idea of the hand is an anthropomorphic image, a human picture to describe an aspect of God, who is a spirit and therefore doesn't have a hand in the sense we understand. This picture conveys an individualized reaching out to hold us personally. God doesn't just dump out a bunch of upholding and hope that we can catch some for ourselves.

If the hand in the text is our own, the personal touch is still there. God doesn't just drop some support out there under our feet or push us from behind; he takes us by our hand to draw us after himself into his purposes and out of dangers.

In these pictures the Lord is both capable of helping us and perfectly willing to do so. This is made explicit in Psalm 62, in which the poet declares this truth:

> One thing God has spoken,
> two things have I heard:
> that you, O God, are strong,
> and that you, O Lord, are loving.
>   *Psalm 62:11–12a*

The poet of Psalm 37 has had ample time to observe these qualities of the Lord. He notes in verse 25, just following our section, that he is now old and has never seen the righteous forsaken. Then, in the next several verses, he continues his words of wisdom to the young, and advises them to turn away from evil and to watch out for the wicked.

The last line of our excerpt, verse 37, summarizes well the message of the psalm. The poet says, literally, "Watch the complete one and see the upright, for there is a posterity to a man of *shalom*." We must remember from Chapter 26 that a person of *shalom* lives in right relationship with God and, therefore, in right relationship with him- or herself and with others.

That kind of person—one who is tranquil and contented and filled and whole—does indeed have a posterity. *Posterity* could refer either specifically to children, as the New English Bible and the Jerusalem Bible translate it, or simply to a future. The word is used sometimes as a poetic parallel to the word *hope*, so it emphasizes that all dimensions of the future look positive for the person of *shalom*.

For this reason, the poet urges his listeners to "consider the blameless." The NASV says to "mark the blameless man." We should use our intelligence to observe what happens to such persons of God, so that we might be inspired by their example. The ones we are to watch are those who are complete—the morally innocent, the ones having integrity.

Similarly, we are to "behold the upright" (NASV), in the sense of perceiving or understanding those who are straightforward. This same word, *upright*, has been used in verse 14 to signify those who are being persecuted by the wicked, but this psalm always emphasizes that they are afflicted only for a little while. These troubles will soon be over, for, ultimately, there is a future for the person of *shalom*.

These verses invite us to be a part of that future, to steady ourselves by listening to Yahweh. When we are silent before him, he is not hindered. Our own solitude can help us learn to be still and listen. The more we observe those who have integrity, the more we will follow their example and rest in the wholeness that Yahweh delights to establish for us.

FOR FURTHER MEDITATION

1. When during the day am I silent to Yahweh?
2. Do I wait longingly for his purposes to be fulfilled? Why or why not?
3. When have I experienced burning out because of vexation? How could I avoid that problem?
4. How have I seen that Yahweh has established my steps?
5. How have I experienced the fact that, though I might fall, I will not be hurled headlong—or, in the words of Paul, "I might be struck down, but never struck out"?
6. What have I learned from the models of persons of integrity?
7. What do I think *posterity* means as it is promised to the person of *shalom?* Why is *shalom* such an important aspect of that concept?

31. So Now I Can't Keep It to Myself

I waited patiently for the LORD;
   he turned to me and heard my cry. . . .
He put a new song in my mouth,
   a hymn of praise to our God.
Many will see and fear
   and put their trust in the LORD.
Blessed is the man
   who makes the LORD his trust,
who does not look to the proud,
   to those who turn aside to false gods.
Many, O LORD my God,
   are the wonders you have done.
The things you planned for us
   no one can recount to you;
were I to speak and tell of them,
   they would be too many to declare.
Sacrifice and offering you did not desire,
   but my ears you have pierced,
burnt offerings and sin offerings
   you did not require.
Then I said, "Here I am, I have come—
   it is written about me in the scroll.
To do your will, O my God, is my desire;
   your law is within my heart."
I proclaim righteousness in the great assembly;
   I do not seal my lips,
   as you know, O LORD.
I do not hide your righteousness in my heart;
   I speak of your faithfulness and salvation.
I do not conceal your love and your trust
   from the great assembly.

Psalm 40:1, 3–10

The LORD uses the circumstances of our lives in funny ways to
speak of his love to others. After ten months of studying the

Psalms, I finally knew the general content of each of them well enough to think about them one at a time while I swam lengths of the pool. On the Tuesday before Thanksgiving I swam through the whole Book of Psalms twice. Though a bit more than four and a quarter miles was an exercise record for me then, the greater value lay in meditating on the Psalms once to review their content and once as a vehicle for prayer. When I finished I felt so exhilarated by the Joy of that meditation time that I kidded with friends about trying to swim seven miles in May—since seven is the biblical number for perfection.

Suddenly it seemed silly to wait until May when I was already in shape for it, so two weeks later I did seven miles. My swimming partner told the local newspaper about my attempt, and they decided, probably because I am a diabetic, to do a "special interest" story. Consequently, when I finished five hundred lengths, I was greeted, not only by a few friends, but also by a photographer and a reporter from the paper, who asked me first why I had done it.

My goals in the swim were to challenge my memory in meditating on the Psalms and to use the Scriptures for emotional healing, as well as to prove my own physical fitness in spite of debilitating handicaps. When the story appeared in the newspaper two days later, the swim also became a wonderful means for speaking to this community about the love of God. Four months later, my ten-mile swim to raise money for the unemployed was an even greater opportunity to bring God's love to bear on a particular problem in our society.

Out of my loneliness came ministry. That has been the story all along. God keeps turning around things that cause me pain and using them as vehicles for evangelism. That is also the message of Psalm 40. This psalm includes a lament—in fact, the lament is repeated almost exactly as the seventieth poem in the Psalter. But Psalm 40 also begins with a hymn of praise as the poet's response to all the good things that God has brought out of his trouble. When David declares that he had waited patiently for the LORD and that Yahweh had turned to him, heard his cry, and lifted him out of the pit, he sets the scene for the praises that follow.

I am ashamed, however, when I read the opening phrase of

the psalm. After all he went through, how could David say, "I waited patiently"? Literally, the Hebrew idiom reads, "to wait for I waited for Yahweh." Its special infinitive absolute form stresses the hope and patience involved, until the waiting ended in deliverance. The result of that deliverance, in turn, was evangelism, which is recorded in several ways that we will consider here.

The first expression of evangelism comes immediately after the poet's description of God's deliverance. He declares that Yahweh "put a new song in my mouth, a hymn of praise to our God." Notice that Yahweh *places* the song in his mouth. That ties in with several New Testament passages which tell us that we do not need to worry about what we will say, for the Holy Spirit will give us the what and the how (see, for example, Matt. 10:19–20). God is in charge of creating our songs; he enables us to praise.

God did put new songs in my mouth when the reporter asked me why I had swum seven miles. Praise came easily because so very obviously the whole situation had been created by God. He had given me the strength to swim and the words to describe it.

Next, David tells us that from a new song of praise "many will see and fear and put their trust in the Lord." After the newspaper article on my swim appeared, a few lonely people called (I had mentioned that I was working on this book on the Psalms). Various friends told me how the story had encouraged them and stimulated their faith. A pastor in town referred to the article in his sermon the next Sunday in order to urge his parishioners to study the Scriptures. In so many ways God can use things we would never expect as vehicles of praise to draw people closer to himself. Some of the new songs he creates might seem odd to us, but he has good purposes behind them.

The fourth verse adds a necessary warning: Blessedness, it declares, lies in making the Lord one's trust, not in turning to the proud or to those falling away to a lie. Some scholars think that the word for "proud" is a scribal error and should read, "the Baalim," which is a name for the false gods of the cultures that surrounded the people of Israel. Possibly this passage is a warning against idolatry, but more likely it is a warning to seek humility.

How easily we forget our proper place! The incident of the newspaper story forced me to recognize the danger of pride when people comment to me about the "great feat" of swimming so far. I am grateful for this psalm's reminder that blessedness lies in making the LORD our trust. The swimming project was intended from the beginning as a way to get to know the LORD better both intellectually and spiritually and to receive his healing for my physical and emotional being. Consequently, I want to make sure that credit goes where credit is due.

The LORD is always to be our trust. We dare never let ourselves get caught up in complacent pride. We must be wary of its temptation. I want to be sure even that my motives in telling you about the swimming incident are to illustrate the ideas of evangelism in this psalm and not to make you think well of me. See what a terrible danger there always is? Satan would certainly like to corrupt everything if he could.

The second warning is against trusting in those "who turn aside to false gods," or as the NIV footnote says, "to falsehood." Manuscript evidence seems to favor the second interpretation. Either way the warning is necessary.

Our culture surrounds us with temptations everywhere to turn to lies. For example, in our society there is much emphasis on physical beauty: The spiritual benefits of swimming meditation times could get lost if I got caught up in the physical benefits. We dare not trust in our physical strength instead of in the LORD. Psalm 147:10–11 is a good caution against that. Those verses say concerning the LORD that "his pleasure is not in the strength of the horse, nor his delight in the legs of a man [or woman—meaning a person's physical prowess]; the LORD delights in those who fear him, who put their hope in his unfailing love." Of course, we are healthier if we stay in shape as much as possible, and God is glorified when we take good care of our bodies, which are his temple (see 1 Cor. 6:19–20). Ultimately, however, physical well-being is not what pleases God about us. The LORD wants us to fear him, to hope in his *chesedh* (see Chapter 1), and to trust in him rather than in ourselves.

I can't rely on my own strength now that I've "proved" it. In fact, as I was thinking through the Book of Psalms that day, I realized more than ever how dependent everything in life is upon the gracious provision of our Father, whose care we desperately need. I became more grateful for my twice-daily insulin injections, which remind me constantly that my life is dependent.

Many other lies in the world tempt us to turn away from trusting in Yahweh. However, the poet shows us, a genuine reflection upon his works will soon turn us back to recognizing his supremacy and the emptiness of the world's deceptions. In the process, we are also turned back again to the theme of evangelism and witness.

When the poet assesses what God has done, he realizes that he has accomplished many wonders. We encountered this noun in Psalm 139 (see Chapter 22). It describes those things that fill a person with awe because they are so extraordinary. God's works appear too hard and difficult for us, so we are filled with amazement. The things that Yahweh has planned for us, "no one can recount," or, as the Hebrew says, literally, "Your thoughts toward us it is not possible to compare."

God's gifts and wonders are too many for us to proclaim. His plans are too great for us to understand. (Compare Isa. 55:8–9.) We can't adequately comprehend them, nor can we thoroughly announce them to the world. His deeds are just too great.

This gives us tremendous confidence as we seek to share our faith. We know how easy it is to talk when we have too much to say. If we see a friend after being apart for a long time and have to catch up on everything, words just come pouring out. In the same way, our witness to the wonders of the LORD's doing comes out of the overflow of our lives. As we observe his wonderful works, with Joy we proclaim them because their magnificence overwhelms us. I was exclaiming about that with one of my newest friends on Thanksgiving. As we talked about God's loving action in our lives, we anticipated using the rest of our lives to keep on learning and sharing such things, yet we will still need all of eternity to comprehend the Joy of it all.

Once again, the poet moves to the negative side as he reminds himself and us that Yahweh does not really desire sacrifices and burnt offerings. The Hebrew word for "offering" specifically refers to grain offerings as opposed to the burnt and sin offerings that are mentioned next. All of these were useful tools for the Chosen People to picture the coming of the One who would be the perfect sacrifice, but they were useful only as tools. The sacrifices themselves could not save the people. Animals and harvests were not really what the LORD wanted from them.

What he wants is still the same today as in the Old Testament times. God longs for us to desire to do his will. He wants his instruction to be so important to us that we eagerly hold it within our hearts. Though the NIV uses the translation "heart," the original Hebrew uses a word that means "the bowels or the inward part" of a person. This word choice emphasizes that God wants us to hold his instruction in that which is the *source* of our emotions. We will not be guided purely subjectively, by our emotions themselves, but it is our will and feelings that will be tempered by his instruction.

When David declares that the instruction of Yahweh is at the very core of his being, I realize how far from that goal I am. God doesn't want our sacrifices. After all, he owns the cattle on a thousand hills, so why would he need our extra bullock? (See Psalm 50:7–10.) He doesn't want our burnt offerings. He wants us. Therefore, Paul urges us to "present our bodies as living sacrifices, holy and pleasing to God—which is your spiritual worship" (Rom. 12:2).

David announces in the middle of verse 6, "but my ears you have pierced." When slaves were set free, yet chose to stay with their masters and serve them, their ears were pierced with an awl to signify their devotion. God would have us choose to serve him gladly, even though his love has set us free. Paul uses this image in the many places where he calls himself the slave of Christ.

Finally, in Psalm 40 the poet moves back to a statement about his witness: He continually proclaims Yahweh's righteousness in the great assembly. As the LORD knows, he does not seal his lips. He does not hide His righteousness, but rather he speaks of His faithfulness, His salvation, His steadfast love, His truth. All these concepts that we have seen throughout the Psalms are the subject of the poet's praise in the great assembly. He is "not ashamed of the gospel," as Paul would say, "for it is the power of God for the salvation of everyone" (Rom. 1:16).

Notice all the poetic repetitions in these last two verses. The poet's witness before the great assembly both begins and ends the sequence. Several similar verbs repeat the idea of not concealing, not hiding, not suppressing. Once we get excited about the righteousness and steadfast love and faithfulness and salvation and truth of our God, it is impossible for us to keep silent about those things. We can't hide them. They must spring forth and be apparent to those around us.

This has been my prayer for you throughout this book. Not only have I wanted to bring God's comfort into your particular life situation against whatever sadness or grief or loneliness oppresses you, but beyond that my deeper goal is that the comfort of the Psalms be passed on through you to others. Many around you suffer from the same kinds of loneliness that you are experiencing. If God has here used the Psalms to touch you with peace and healing, then let me encourage you to proclaim in the great assembly what he has done. His wonders are, after all, too many to recount.

If we all get started now telling others about his wonderful works on our behalf, we won't be finished by the time we get to heaven. And there we will perfectly praise him, even as there we will perfectly know his comfort and hope and peace. Then we will proclaim his truth and faithfulness and righteousness and salvation and steadfast love into all eternity. There in Joy we will never be lonely again, and the LORD himself will wipe away all the tears from our eyes.

FOR FURTHER MEDITATION

1. What new songs has the LORD given me to sing lately? What new songs have I discovered since I started reading this book?

2. How have others come to know the LORD more deeply through the new songs in my heart?

3. How have I experienced loss of blessedness when I have become proud?

4. How have I experienced loss of blessedness when I have turned to the deceptions or lies of the world around me or the false gods that can't give me the security for which I am longing?

5. What happens to my feelings when I realize that God's blessings are too many to count or to begin to declare to others?

6. If God does not desire sacrifice and offerings, what is the place for them in our Christian lives? How do they fit in with what he does want—for us to want his will?

7. What opportunities do I have to speak his praises in the great assembly? How would I like to create new ways to do so?

Appendix A:
Swimming the Psalms*

My best meditation on the Word happens in the swimming pool. Now don't immediately stop reading this chapter because you're thinking, "But I don't like to swim" or "On what verses do I meditate while I'm drowning?" The point is that I have found great value in linking together my spiritual and physical disciplines. My desire for both is strengthened, and the benefits of both seem to be increased.

I pray that this description of personal Bible study habits that have been helpful to me will stimulate your own thinking, that perhaps you might get some new ideas for your own quiet times. I don't share my experience as an expert, however; in fact, my very need to link Scripture meditation with a physical discipline is probably a sign of my own weakness—I'm not sure. In any case, such a connection works for me.

As a free-lance Bible teacher, I became very frustrated that I often said to people, "Turn to the Psalms; they include every human emotion and can be vastly comforting in every situation," but I did not know the Psalms well enough to be able to suggest in particular situations which specific Psalms might be helpful. At the same time, I was bored with lap swimming. It is necessary for my health for me to work out vigorously several times each week, but the miles of laps back and forth in the same water dragged on interminably. After thinking about the idea only superficially for several months, I finally took the plunge and began to be serious about learning to know the Psalms better. The methods that have evolved over half a year have brought such Joy to me that I'm eager to tell you about them.

*Copyright © 1981, *The Bible Newsletter*, 1716 Spruce St., Philadelphia, PA 19103.

My morning quiet times at home begin with the reading of the next psalm, after which I read about that psalm in *The Layman's Bible Commentary* (vol. 9 [Richmond, Va.: John Knox Press, 1960]). Then I read the psalm again to follow its structure and to pick out key verses or ones that particularly strike me. At scattered moments throughout the day and in the weeks to come, I work on memorizing these verses. All of this information is gathered in a meditation notebook. For each psalm I record a title and the kind of psalm that it is, such as an individual or community thanksgiving or lament, a hymn of praise, an affirmation of faith, and so forth. These classifications are well introduced and listed in the commentary. Next in my notebook I put an outline of the psalm and then the verses that I have selected to memorize. This is the material for the pool meditation.

The importance of the notebook emphasizes a significant distinction between two elements that have greatly deepened my growth in the Scriptures. The morning time of writing in the notebook is *study.* When I am swimming and thinking, that study provides the basis for my *meditation.* During the first lap, I think about the first psalm. That happens to be one that I have memorized entirely, so I usually recite it as I stroke down the lane, but sometimes I think about ways in which I have fallen into the company of the godless or how blessed it is to delight in the instruction of the LORD. On lap two I think about the second psalm, and so on.

For some of the psalms I have learned songs. To sing those songs while I swim is a good way for me to spend time simply praising God in his own words. Other psalms touch off prayers for particular people. For example, Psalms 14 and 53, which are almost exactly alike, speak of fools who say there is no God. Usually those two laps are filled with prayers for people, especially some friends of mine, who haven't yet come to know Christ. Lap twenty-two, which uses a slower, resting backstroke in my warm-up routine, gives me extra time to think about all the images of the passion of Christ in Psalm 22.

I have been adding a psalm each day for several months, so now it takes more than a mile and a quarter to think about them all. I have seen that my body is getting stronger even as is my spirit. My goal is to be ready to swim the whole Book of Psalms by Thanksgiving.

All sorts of exciting results have come out of studying the Psalms in this way. First of all, I really am learning them better, and that has been helpful for my own times of discouragement, as well as for counseling. Now, instead of paging through the Bible trying to find something that is comforting, I know which of the psalms are appropriate to whatever I might be encountering.

Also, I am amazed at the constant newness of the Scriptures. It astounds me that a psalm that I've been meditating upon for several months yields new insights at each fresh approach. One delightful experience of that freshness happened the day I'd come to Psalm 90. I was so thrilled by what I'd learned in my meditations that morning that I did all ninety again, and then I was filled with such wonder that I'd learned even more new things on the second time through that I swam through them all a third time. Once again the Psalms spoke to me in yet more new ways. I was so excited that I wasn't even tired, though I had swum four miles for the first time in my life. God's Word is indeed a treasure chest.

It is essential for me to look over my notebook frequently, because verses that I have chosen get forgotten after many weeks. I try to keep refreshing my memory so that the Spirit has plenty of material to work with as he nudges my thoughts in various directions proceeding from those things that he brings to my mind.

Another benefit of studying the Psalms in this way has been a deepened appreciation of the Word in formal worship settings. I belong to a Lutheran church, which frequently uses psalms in the structured services. When a psalm is simply read or a section of one is chanted as part of the liturgy, I experience it much more deeply because I have spent many laps thinking about the meanings and applications of that psalm.

A new benefit of such meditation just opened up for me two days ago. A dear friend, whose kidneys failed several years ago, met with his doctor to discuss the advantages and disadvantages of changing to a new method of dialysis. The decision that my friend had to make between his present treatment and a new type of treatment would greatly affect his time, appearance, and potential for work and ministry. I promised Tim that I would support him in prayer all the while he was at the doctor's office.

At first I thought that I would have to skip my Psalms meditations for the day, but those very excerpts from the Psalms proved to be magnificent vehicles for my prayers. I have never prayed for one person for two hours before, and it was a Joy-filled experience! For example, as I swam the fourth lap, I thought of the verse, "Know that the Lord has set apart the godly for himself; the Lord will hear when I call to him" (4:3). That led me to thank God that he has set Tim apart as a sacred vessel and that I could trust him to guide Tim's decision so that he would choose the best means of treatment for God's purposes.

Suddenly, in connection with one of the psalms, it hit me that I had been praying for Tim to choose the treatment that would best affect his ministry to his family and friends and in his church, but I had not at all prayed about which treatment would be best for his own personal growth in relationship with the Lord. Then, Psalm 81 led me to think about the various false gods that could affect his decision—idols of appearance or security or our culture's valuing of people according to the status of their jobs. It took me several laps to pray through all that I discovered about idolatry, and that led to some serious thinking later that afternoon about the false gods in my own life.

The whole process gave me many new insights into my friend's situation and caused me to praise God in so many new ways for who He is and for the gift of Tim and for His actions in His people's lives. I don't think I had ever realized so powerfully before how directly connected to our present-day experiences and twentieth-century decisions the words of the Scriptures are. Finally, one of the greatest Joys for me was that Tim felt thoroughly enfolded in an assurance of truth and the love of God the whole time that he weighed the decision. The word had been the vehicle for my prayers and his trust.

You might be wondering how any of this could be applied to your own devotional life. Perhaps the following principles drawn from the illustrations above will suggest some ideas for you to try:

1. Times of physical exercise—such solo activities as jogging, calisthenics, isometrics, walking, bicycling, housecleaning, or swimming—can be good times for thinking about the Scriptures.

2. Time spent in study prior to the opportunity for meditation provides food for our thoughts.

3. It is spiritually enriching simply to praise God in his own words, to reflect on his character and its meaning for our lives.

4. The better we know the Scriptures, the more use we can make of them for comfort and sustenance in the tough times.

5. An open mind allows God constantly to be teaching us new things from the passages of his word upon which we meditate.

6. Meditation on passages of the Scriptures that are used in liturgical services makes them more significant in our worship experiences.

7. Meditation on the word is an excellent basis for our prayers. The Scriptures reveal to us the character of God and teach us how we can turn to him. They enable us to be specific about our requests.

Appendix B:
When Is a Rut Not a Rut?
Hidden Promise in Psalm 23*

There is more than one way to be in a rut.

As I rode my bike though the woods, I kept trying to stay out of the deep rut made, I suppose, by a motorcycle. Frustration mounted as I continued to lose my balance, to get my tires stuck, and to waste a lot of energy trying to make progress. But when I finally gave up fighting that awful rut and chose instead to ride along in it, I was amazed at the ease and pleasure that resulted. As long as I was careful to stay in the midst of what had now become a "track" to me, I didn't get mired in mud or snagged by dead branches. I was more free to enjoy the scenery and to pedal with more power. Whether the path was a "rut" or a "track" depended upon my choice and the perspective that resulted.

So it is with the way of the Lord. I was excited to learn recently that the Hebrew word that we translate "paths" in Psalm 23:3 ("He leads me in paths of righteousness for his name's sake") actually means "tracks." The word comes from a Hebrew verb root that means "to roll" something that is round. From this verb is derived the noun that signifies a "cart" and, consequently, the word used in Psalm 23:3 for an "entrenchment" or "wagon-track."

The term is used figuratively in the Scriptures to mean "the snares of the wicked" (Ps. 140:6) or "a course of action or life" (Prov. 4:26). Since in Psalm 23:3 the word occurs together with the noun for "that which is right," we know that the tracks meant in this verse are a positive course of action.

---

*Reprinted by permission of *Eternity* Magazine, copyright © 1980, Evangelical Ministries, Inc., 1716 Spruce Street, Philadelphia, PA 19103.

Psalm 23 begins, of course, with the assurance that the Lord is a faithful Shepherd, who feeds and provides rest and refreshment for his flock. But he doesn't carry the sheep in the path that they should travel. He *leads* them. They could choose not to follow if they wanted. The parable of Jesus about the one who goes astray (Matt. 18:12–14) indicates that even some who are members of the flock might wander away. We each must choose what we want to do about our Shepherd's leading.

Two other phrases in the psalm add insight to our understanding of the meaning of the Lord's leading us in the tracks of righteousness. The one I want to study with you first was a surprising discovery for me because of the misunderstanding created by a romanticized interpretation of this psalm. In verse 4, the phrase, "thy rod and thy staff, they comfort me," is usually thought of in soft and gentle terms. We like to hear the word *comfort* as if it were meant to make us comfortable. Recently I read in the Navigators' *Daily Walk* Bible-reading program this arresting sentence: "God does not comfort us to make us comfortable, but to make us comforters."

When we read this phrase in Psalm 23, we must remember that the rod was used by the shepherd for beating or smiting— for chastisement. It was a club, not a feather! The implication is that sometimes the sheep need to be dealt with sternly to keep them in the tracks of righteousness.

We might wonder how that could be comforting. The Hebrew construction of the phrase almost seems to be directed toward our doubts. It adds an extra pronoun *they* in order to say, "thy rod and thy staff—*they* are comforting me." David seems to be assuring us, "Yes, indeed! What actually appears to be painful to you is in reality the source of comfort."

That makes a lot of sense to me! Recently my life was being torn up by great turmoil and personal crisis. Some days the pain seemed too great as I moved into new work outside of the parish I had been serving and as I battled several dimensions of deterioration in my health. Yet, above all the anguish came this promise: The rod is a source of comfort! Sufferings are meant to help me to follow the Shepherd in the tracks of righteousness. Yes, indeed! It was good to know that my wise Shepherd loved me so much that he allowed those dimensions of difficulty to keep me in the right tracks.

Just as the jarring of the rough edge reminded me I needed to concentrate on keeping my bicycle in the center of the tracks, so I needed the discipline of the Shepherd's rod to remind me to watch carefully how he leads. I don't want to wander from the tracks of his righteousness. I want him to change me, to conform me to the image of the perfect Lamb.

The other phrase that further defines the nature of this entrenchment is this final thought from verse 3: "for his name's sake." The phrase means "for the purpose of vindicating his name, of maintaining his reputation or character consistently."

What a privilege! Our Shepherd leads us in tracks that will show his character to be consistent. In other words, if his people stay in the tracks of his right ways of behaving, they will be witnesses to dimensions of this Shepherd's character. If they remain loving in the face of brutal opposition or persecution, they will maintain the reputation of a God of love. If they suffer calamity with calmness and trust, they will reveal their Shepherd to be a God of strength and grace. Again I say, what a privilege!

Our God has been revealed to us as such a God—of love and strength and grace. In our times of discipline we have the honor of passing that revelation on to those around us. Surely His goodness and mercy will follow us if that is the choice of our life! We will indeed dwell in the Lord's house forever because he has kept us in his path. And we will have invited others to join us in his house because we have revealed the goodness of his tracks to them by our choosing to remain in them.

There is more than one way to be in a rut. To be in the rut of sin, despair, and rebellion against the purposes of God leads to death. Yet, our Shepherd calls us to follow him in the tracks of righteousness. We are guided and comforted there by the rod of his chastisement. The results of staying in those tracks are glory to him, as his character is shown to be consistent, and Joy to us, as we experience the consequent freedom, power, and blessings of pasture and rest.

List of Resources

WORKS CITED

Leupold, H. C. *Exposition of Psalms*. Reprint. Grand Rapids, Mich.: Baker Book House, 1969.

Rhodes, Arnold B. *The Book of Psalms*. Vol. 9 of *The Layman's Bible Commentary*, edited by Balmer H. Kelly. Richmond, Va.: John Knox Press, 1960.

Richards, Lawrence O. *69 Ways to Start a Study Group and Keep It Growing*. Grand Rapids, Mich.: Zondervan, 1973.

Sabath, Jackie. "Euclid Street Journal: A Wedding Sermon." *Sojourners*. Vol. 10, no. 11 (November 1981), pp. 24–25.

Sedore, Marva J. *To Walk and Not Faint*. Chappaqua, N.Y.: Christian Herald Books, 1980.

Welter, Paul. *How to Help a Friend*. Wheaton, Ill: Tyndale House, 1978.

White, John. *The Tower of Geburah*. Downers Grove, Ill: Inter-Varsity Press, 1978.

OTHER WORKS

Some unusual works on the Psalms that I have found very helpful are these:

Brandt, Leslie F. *Psalms/Now*. St. Louis, Mo.: Concordia, 1973.

Briscoe, Stuart. *What Works When Life Doesn't: Practical Help from the Psalms*. Wheaton, Ill.: Victor Books, 1976.

Lewis, C. S. *Reflections on the Psalms*. New York: Harcourt, Brace & World, 1958.

Peterson, Eugene H. *A Long Obedience in the Same Direction: Discipleship in an Instant Society*. Downers Grove, Ill.: Inter-Varsity Press, 1980.

Other excellent commentaries besides the two listed above:

Kidner, Derek. *Psalms 1–72* and *Psalms 73–150*. Vols. 14a and 14b of the *Tyndale Old Testament Commentaries*. D. J. Wiseman, gen. ed. Downers Grove, Ill.: Inter-Varsity Press, 1973.

Spurgeon, C. H. *The Treasury of David: An Expository and Devotional Commentary on the Psalms*. 7 vols. Grand Rapids, Mich.: Baker Book House, 1977.

Subject Index

Aaron, 168
Abimelech, 72, 78
Abortion, 128
Acceptance-with-Joy, 177
Achish, 72
Acrostic, psalm as, 72–73, 170
Adam, 144
Adonai, meaning of word, 7, 161
Amen, meaning of word, 17
Angels, 79–81, 150–151
Asaph, 101, 102, 107, 111, 113, 114, 115, 117

Betrayal, handling, 40–41
Bible study: discipline of, 21, 31, 51; guidelines for, 191–195
Blessedness, to those who seek the Lord, 83, 87
Boasting, right kind of, 72–76
Book, meaning of word, 55
Brutish, ourselves as, 107–112

Chesedh of God, 4–6, 27, 60, 75, 98, 115, 165, 185
Colson, Chuck, 174
Comfort, without assurance, 156–162
Commit, meaning of word, 16–17
Consolation of God, 99–100
Corporate worship, importance of, 143–148
Covenant God, 8, 140, 159, 166
Creation, magnificence of, 126–127
Crushed in spirit, meaning of term, 91

David, 2, 3, 26, 36, 42, 48, 57, 66, 72, 73, 74, 77, 78, 82, 83, 84, 85, 87, 91, 93, 109, 132, 134, 135, 153, 159, 162, 183, 184, 187
Death, God's help in, 118–124
Delight, in God, 99, 172

Desires of heart, God to give, 170–174
Desiring nothing on earth, 113–117
Despair, psalms of, 157–160

Elisha, 80
Envy of wicked, how to avoid, 101–106
Ephesus Community, 55, 142
Escape, longing for, 36–37
Eschatology, 114
Eternal perspective, to avoid envy of wicked, 105–106
Evangelism, 75, 82, 182–188
Eve, 144

Faithfulness of God, 28, 78
Families, lonely set in, 137–142
Fear: handling, 48–53; as reverence or honor, 83–84; right kind of, 59–64
Fellowship, discipline of, 72
Flood, 152–153
Friends, help of in resisting temptation, 135–136

God: as answering cries of panic, 13–18, 95–100; *chesedh* of, 4–6, 27, 60, 75, 98, 115, 165, 185; consolation of, 99–100; as Covenant God, 8, 140, 159, 166; faithfulness of, 28, 78; as having design for us, 129; as loving us in our brutishness, 107–112; mother-love of, 25–29, 110; as near, 89–94; as noticing our wanderings, 54–55; as recording our tears, 54–58; as releasing us from our snares, 31–35; as righteous, 120; as rock, 116; as Shepherd, 198–199; tasting goodness of, 82–87; trustworthiness of, 8–11, 64, 171

Godly: meaning of word, 60; as separated out, 60–61

Hannah, 140
Hearing: meaning of word, 45; relation to joy, 74
Heart, meaning of word, 67, 107, 133, 164, 187
Hind's Feet on High Places, 177
Historical perspective for grief and loneliness, 163–168
Hope: God to restore, 89–94; meaning of word, 146, 161
How to Help a Friend, 82
Hurnard, Hannah, 177

Isaiah, 170

Jacob, 167
James, 154
Joseph, 167, 168
Joshua, 168
Joy: relation to hearing, 74; through Easter, 66–71

Kidneys, meaning of word, 107, 126

Law, purpose of, 62
The Layman's Bible Commentary, 138
Left hand, significance of, 110
Levi, 147
Lewis, C. S., 92
Life after death, in Old Testament, 113–114
Light, concept of, 146
Loneliness, 1–2, 4–6, 13, 19, 20, 25, 29, 34, 44–45, 60, 72, 75, 97, 118–119, 150, 157, 165, 170, 183
Lord. See God
Lord's Supper, 83
Luther, Martin, 62

MAP International, 174
Mary, 80, 140
Meditation: discipline of, 21, 31; guidelines for, 191–195
Miracles, meaning of word, 167
Moses, 77, 168
Mother-love, of God, 25–29, 110

Nephesh, meaning of, 20, 73–74

Pain, problem of, 40
Panic, help from God in, 13–18, 95–100
Patience, 177
Paul, 22, 27, 57, 64, 68, 69, 73, 78, 79, 84, 87, 91, 105, 110, 114, 122, 123, 131, 132, 138, 179, 187
Peter, 45, 47, 110
Pharisees, 113
Phillips, J. B., 179
Prayer, discipline of, 21, 31, 72, 132
Prison Fellowship, 174

Radiance, of people of God, 77
Realized eschatology, 114
Refuge, meaning of word, 16
Relinquishment, ethic of, 116
Rest, importance of 38
Resurrection, Joy through, 66–71
Richards, Larry, 48
Righteous, God as, 120
Right hand, significance of, 110, 111
Rock, as figure for God, 116
Rod and staff, comfort of, 198–199

Sadducees, 113
Safety, related to trust, 70. See also Security
Saints, Christians as, 84, 119
Sanctuaries, meaning of word, 104
Satan, power of, 92, 132
Saul, 72
Scripture, study of. See Bible study
Security: in God, 171–172; relation to trust, 8. See also Safety
Selah, 38–39, 63, 165, 167
Seraphim, meaning of word, 80–81
Seven, significance of, 152
Sexual temptation, resisting, 131–136
Shakespeare, William, 125
Shalom, 70, 150, 153–154, 176–181
Shepherd, God as, 198–199
Sin, meaning of, 26
69 Ways to Start a Study Group and Keep It Growing, 48
Snares, God to release us from, 31–35
Sojourners, 115
Sojourners community, 52
Solitary, meaning of word, 33

Solitude, importance of, 38
Sons of Korah, 147
Soul, meaning of, 20, 73–74
Special, ourselves as, 125–130
Spirit, meaning of word, 164–165
Splendor, meaning of word, 151
Staff and rod, comfort of, 198–199
Strength, finding, 149–155
Support groups, 74
Sustain, meaning of word, 46
Swimming, as meditation time, 31, 59, 182–183, 191–195

Tasting goodness of the Lord, 82–87
Tears, as recorded by God, 54–58
Temptation, resisting, 131–136
Teresa, Mother, 174
Think, meaning of word, 164
Time, God in control of, 7–12
The Tower of Geburah, 85, 90, 110, 134
Transgressions, meaning of word, 27, 161

Travail, 103
Troubles, as increasing with faith, 92
Trust: in God, 8–11, 64, 171; related to safety, security, 8, 70

Uphold, God to, 179

Wallis, Jim, 52
Wanderings, God as noticing our, 54–55
Welter, Paul, 82
Western Evangelical Seminary, 143
"What Wondrous Love Is This," 62
Wholeness, 153–154
Witnessing, 182–188. *See also* Evangelism
World Vision hospital, 174
Worship, importance of, 143–148

Yahweh, meaning of word, 7–8. *See also* God

Zechariah, 80

Scripture Index

OLD TESTAMENT

Genesis **2:7**, 20
Exodus **32:11–14**, 22; **34:29–35**, 77
Numbers **6:26**, 67
Joshua **4:6–7**, 168
1 Samuel **2:1**, 140; **21:10–22:2**, 72
2 Kings **6:8–23**, 80; **6:16**, 80; **6:17**, 80
1 Chronicles **6**, 147; **16:24**, 151
2 Chronicles **20:21**, 151
Nehemiah **8:10b**, 75
Job **19:25–27**, 113
Psalms **4**, 59, 66; **4:1b–2**, 66; **4:3**, 194; **4:3–5**, 59–64; **4:4**, 70; **4:4–5**, 59–64; **4:6**, 67; **4:6–8**, 66–71; **4:8**, 70; **13:1–6**, 2, 4, 6; **13:3–4**, 3; **14**, 192; **16:5**, 117; **16:8**, 109; **16:11**, 113; **22**, 32, 192; **22:1–3a**, 157; **23**, 197–199; **23:3**, 112, 197, 199; **23:4**, 198; **24:4**, 20; **25**, 20; **25:1–2**, 19–23; **25:6–7**, 25–29; **25:8**, 28; **25:9**, 28; **25:10**, 25–29, 28, 29; **25:11**, 29; **25:15**, 34; **25:15–18**, 30–35; **28:2**, 16; **28:6**, 16; **29**, 149, 150, 154; **29:1–5a**, 149–155; **29:8a**, 149–155; **29:9c–11**, 149–155; **30**, 31; **31**, 8, 13; **31:4**, 112; **31:5**, 13–18, 16; **31:14–15a**, 7–12; **31:22**, 13–18, 14, 15; **34**, 72, 79; **34:1**, 109; **34:1–3**, 72–76; **34:3**, 74; **34:5**, 85; **34:5–7**, 77–81; **34:7**, 83; **34:8**, 82; **34:8–10**, 82–87; **34:9**, 83; **34:11**, 89–94, 93; **34:17**, 92; **34:17–19**, 89–94; **34:18**, 89; **34:19**, 92; **37**, 170, 180; **37:3**, 173; **37:3–6**, 170–174; **37:5**, 173; **37:7**, 176–181; **37:23**, 178; **37:23–24**, 176–181; **37:25**, 180; **37:37**, 176–181, 180; **39**, 157, 158, 159; **39:2–8a**, 156–162; **39:4**, 159; **39:5**, 161; **39:6**, 161; **39:7**, 161; **39:10–13**, 156–162; **39:11**, 161; **40**, 183, 187; **40:1**, 182–188; **40:3–10**, 182–188; **40:6**, 187; **42**, 144, 146; **42:1–2**, 143–148; **42:5**, 144, 161; **42:11**, 144, 161; **43**, 144; **43:3**, 146; **43:3–5**, 143–148; **43:5**, 112, 144, 161; **46**, 97; **46:10**, 63; **50:7–10**, 187; **53**, 192; **55**, 38, 48; **55:6–8**, 36–41; **55:7–8**, 39; **55:12–14**, 36–41; **55:16–17**, 42–47; **55:17**, 43; **55:20–21**, 40, 42; **55:22**, 42–47, 43, 45, 46; **56**, 41, 48, 64; **56:3**, 51; **56:3–4**, 48–53, 53; **56:4**, 51, 57; **56:8–9**, 54–58; **56:8–11**, 54–58; **56:9**, 57; **56:10–11**, 57; **62:11–12a**, 180; **68**, 138, 139; **68:4–6**, 137–142, 139; **68:18**, 138; **68:24–27**, 138; **68:35**, 137–142; **73**, 101, 109, 115, 117; **73:1–5**, 101–106; **73:6**, 103; **73:13**, 101–106, 103; **73:16–17**, 101–106; **73:17**, 104; **73:21–24a**, 107–112; **73:22**, 108; **73:23**, 110; **73:24a**, 111; **73:24–25**, 110; **73:24b**, 113; **73:24b–26**, 113–117; **73:26**, 116; **77**, 134, 164; **77:5–15**, 163–168; **81**, 194; **86:6**, 16; **86:15**, 120; **88**, 157, 160; **88:15–18**, 157; **90**, 193; **94**, 97; **94:16–19**, 95–100, 96; **96:9**, 151; **103**, 27; **103:8**, 120; **103:13**, 8; **104**, 27; **105**, 27; **111–117**, 139; **116**, 119, 120; **116:3–7**, 118–124; **116:4**, 120; **116:7**, 122; **116:15**, 118–124, 122; **119:10**, 99; **130:2**, 16; **139**, 125, 126, 186; **139:10**, 112; **139:13**, 128; **139:13–18**, 125–130; **139:14a**, 128; **140:6**, 197; **141**, 132; **141:1–5**, 131–136; **141:3**, 133; **141:5**, 135; **146–150**, 139; **147:10–11**, 185

Proverbs **4:26**, 197
Isaiah **6**, 62, 80, 84; **30:21**, 10; **40:6**,
   116; **40:8**, 116; **49:13–15**, 8; **55:8–**
9, 186; **55:10–11**, 12; **66:12**, 99
Jeremiah **31:34**, 26

NEW TESTAMENT

Matthew **1:21**, 91; **5:26**, 133; **10:19–
20**, 184; **13:52**, 144; **18:12–14**,
198; **26:36–44**, 37
Luke **1**, 80; **1:47**, 140; **12:4–7**, 52;
14, 80; **16**, 80; **20:27–40**, 114;
22:69, 110; **23:34**, 32; **23:46**, 17
John **1:1–14**, 50; **3:36a**, 105; **3:36**,
114; **8:31**, 18; **8:32**, 18; **8:36**, 18;
10:1–3, 8; **10:11–16**, 8; **10:29**, 130;
14:18, 142; **19:30**, 17
Acts **23:6–11**, 114
Romans **1:16**, 187; **5:1–11**, 73; **5:5**,
161; **5:8**, 62; **8**, 126; **8:18**, 69, 123;
8:28, 69, 123, 129; **8:31b–32**, 57;
12:1, 64; **12:1–2**, 167; **12:2**, 187
1 Corinthians **5:17**, 11; **6:19–20**,
185; **8:3**, 126; **10:13**, 79

2 Corinthians **3:7–13**, 77; **3:18**, 78;
4:8–9, 179
Galatians **2:9**, 110
Ephesians **2:6**, 105; **3:12**, 33; **4:7**,
138; **4:22–24**, 22; **4:26**, 63; **5:20**,
44; **6**, 131–132; **6:12**, 80, 92
Philippians **1:23**, 122; **3:7–11**, 73;
4:4, 68, 75; **4:11b**, 87
1 Thessalonians **5:18**, 44
1 Timothy **2:4**, 123
2 Timothy **2:13**, 27; **4:6–8**, 123
Hebrews **4:14**, 41; **4:14–16**, 158;
4:15, 37
James **2:14–16**, 154
1 Peter **1:8**, 140; **3:15**, 123; **5:7**, 42,
45, 47
Revelation **2:8–11**, 123; **2:10–11**, 17